Trade Credit and Financing Instruments

Trade Credit and Financing Instruments

Lucia Gibilaro

BEP BUSINESS EXPERT PRESS

Trade Credit and Financing Instruments
Copyright © Business Expert Press, LLC, 2019.

First published in 2019 by
Business Expert Press, LLC
222 East 46th Street, New York, NY 10017
www.businessexpertpress.com

ISBN-13: 978-1-94897-601-5 (paperback)
ISBN-13: 978-1-94897-602-2 (e-book)

Business Expert Press Finance and Financial Management Collection

Collection ISSN: 2331-0049 (print)
Collection ISSN: 2331-0057 (electronic)

Cover and interior design by S4Carlisle Publishing Services Private Ltd., Chennai, India

First edition: 2019

10 9 8 7 6 5 4 3 2 1

Printed in the United States of America.

Dedication

The best of me is because of you.

Abstract

Trade credit is extensively used in both domestic and international commercial transactions. Although it clearly supports growth, its significance is even greater for developed countries, where the market has recovered remarkably since the global financial crisis. The number and heterogeneity of motivations to trade credit justify the variability observed in the data on global trading, and the role of trade credit has become crucial in supply chain coordination. A range of diverse trade credit finance solutions are available and include products and services offered by financial intermediaries and market products, highlighting a very interesting set of intermediate solutions that have emerged as a result of new technologies utilized in financial services. For financiers trade credit is an attractive option, but an in-depth evaluation of the possibility of losses forms the basis of a deep understating of numerous sources that can create credit risk (default and dilution risk). This book offers managers a complete analysis of the various facets of commercial credit and presents an analysis of the various types of markets, instruments, and risks associated with trade credit in supply chains across the globe.

Keywords

Asset-based lending; capital requirements; concentration; corporate distress; credit risk; credit risk management; financial market; financing solution; international trade; relationship lending; supply chain; trade credit

Brief Contents

Introduction ....*xiii*

Chapter 1   Trade Credit around the Globe 1

Chapter 2   Trade Credit: Theory and Empirical Evidence 33

Chapter 3   Trade Credit Financing Instruments..............................53

Chapter 4   Credit Risk Framework for Trade Credit Financing
             Exposure 75

Conclusions *93*

References..*97*

About the Author..*113*

Index *115*

Contents

Introduction ....*xiii*

Chapter 1   Trade Credit around the Globe 1

          Introduction 1

          Trade Credit around the World 2

          Industry Segmentation 6

          Segmentation by Firm Type 16

          Synthesis: Multidimensional Segmentation 20

          Conclusions 31

Chapter 2   Trade Credit: Theory and Empirical Evidence 33

          Introduction 33

          Trade Credit across Economic Sectors 34

          Corporate Characteristics and Trade

          Credit Motivation 35

                Real Motivations 35

                Financial Motivation 38

          The Role of Trade Credit in Coordinating

          Business Relationships.......................................41

          Trade Credit and Economic Development 45

          Trade Credit during the Financial Crisis............48

          Conclusions 51

Chapter 3   Trade Credit Financing Instruments................53

          Introduction 53

          Trade Credit Financing Instruments: A Taxonomy 54

                Bank Instruments 54

                Self-Liquidating Loans.............................*54*

                Factoring...*55*

                International Trade Instruments.................*57*

                Supply Chain Finance Instruments............*60*

Market Instruments 65

Commercial Papers 65

Securitization of Receivables 66

Crowdfunding 67

Trade Credit and Self-Liquidating Exposure:

The Relevance of the Debtor 69

Legal Characteristics 69

Operational Characteristics 72

Conclusions 73

Chapter 4   Credit Risk Framework for Trade Credit Financing

Exposure 75

Introduction 75

Credit Risk Framework for Trade Credit

Financial Instruments 76

Credit Risk Evaluation at the Individual Level 77

Default Risk 77

Dilution Risk 80

Credit Risk Evaluation at the Portfolio Level:

Concentration Risk 86

Conclusions 90

Conclusions 93

References 97

About the Author 113

Index 115

Introduction

The life of a business is inextricably tied to the origination of trade credit, a relationship that has withstood the test of time, since trade credit is now extensively used in both international and domestic transactions in developed and developing countries. Therefore, the financing of trade credit is still a requirement for enterprises and an important area for developing markets such as those who could wither and bounce back strongly from the 2008 global financial crisis. In light of the slim chances of trade credit becoming an outdated topic, the evolution of the environment in which trade credit can be utilized has been accompanied by the identification of trade credit's new roles due to its flexible nature. The evolution of technology has expanded the scope of trade credit financing, and, as a consequence, market dynamics are characterized by the emergence of new providers, customers, and products.

The range of solutions to finance trade credit is fairly diversified, ranging from offers by financial intermediaries to offers from new or developing markets; in this scenario, a very interesting set of intermediate solutions have come about because of the use of new technologies in financial services. Despite the regulatory barriers of credit markets at the global level, banks and financial intermediaries have been pressurized to enter into cooperative agreements with enterprise groups connected through either corporate control or business relationships (Global Supply Chain Finance Forum 2016).

Assuming brisk market demand for trade credit financing, it is very important to delve into the motivations of the interest of new providers. A distinctive role for financiers can be identified in the credit risk mitigation determined by trade credit, such that more recent financing solutions based on crowd-lending have enabled retail investors' investment in trade credits (Zhang et al. 2016). The recognition of the possibility of credit risk mitigation associated with trade credit for financiers requires a deeper understanding of credit risk sources, that is, default risk and credit risk, and the relationship between these two categories of risks. Consequently, financiers faced obstacles in developing a full understanding of the underwritten risks in regards to the supplier–debtor relationship. Moreover, because by financing trade credit financiers can end up creating sustained exposure arising from preexisting supply relationships, it is crucial to understand through the vast amount of information available about the circumstances under which such concentrated exposures can threaten the stability of financing sources. The impact of such an understanding can be felt quite strongly, given the support trade credit extends to the economic growth of developing countries (Fisman and Love 2003) and the share of trade credit in the total assets of medium-sized enterprises in select sectors in developed countries (Carbo Valverde et al. 2016).

The findings presented in this book address risk mitigation for trade credit financiers in a global context. Chapter 1 examines the relevance of the topic by measuring different groups of countries' access to trade credit in global trade and later focuses on G7 countries, whose results are presented based on geographical area and type of industry. Focusing on European countries, the chapter analyzes the importance of trade credit based on the criteria of firm size. A multidimensional analysis of trade credit is then presented based on three categories: country, sector, and firm size. Trade credits are not uniform, and their ability to mitigate risk depends on the determinants of their origination. Chapter 2 thus presents a detailed review of both the theoretical and empirical literature on the motivations for recourse to trade credit. Starting with traditional theories based on economic sector and corporate characteristics, the chapter reveals a more recent role of trade credit in coordinating business relationships. The literature on the supporting the practice of extending trade credit to boost growth is then reviewed, and the chapter ends with a special discussion on trade credit during the global financial crisis.

Over the years, solutions to trade credit financing have evolved significantly, broadening the categories of potential financiers and determining their associated risk exposure. After presenting a taxonomy, Chapter 3 discusses in detail bank and market instruments and the implications of legal and operational characteristics for the effectiveness of risk mitigation through debtors' credit reimbursements.

After presenting an institutional and market analysis on trade credit, Chapter 4 takes the reader to a credit risk framework for understanding the trade credit financing exposure at both the individual and portfolio levels. There are two perspectives that this chapter uses to help readers understand risk characteristics. The first one focuses on the dual nature of credit risk in the context of financing of supply chains; default risk and dilution risk are also analyzed, with a discussion on potential overlaps and where to look for information that can be used to evaluate such overlaps. The second perspective focuses on risk concentration, and the implications of a single-name and sectorial/geographic approaches in trade credit financing are discussed.

CHAPTER 1

Trade Credit around the Globe

Introduction

Trade credit originates from the development of business relationships, and new motivations for using trade credit have been discovered over time. The flexibility and up-to-date attributes of trade credit in addressing multifaceted needs emphasize its diversified nature. A uniform approach to the analysis would thus overlook the richness of the information that can be extracted from the segmented analysis of firms' recourse to trade credit. Such information is deemed particularly useful for trade credit financiers in appreciating the potential for growth and the selection of proper financing instruments in a changing environment.

This chapter presents an analysis of trade credit at the international level. First, since the assessment of trade credit in international transactions is still an issue due to the lack of availability of data, a long-term estimation has been obtained by identifying the contributions of different groups of countries that differ geographically as well as in terms of economic development (see Trade Credit around the World section). Since geography alone cannot sufficiently explain trade credit usage, further segmentation by industry is proposed for developed countries (see Industry Segmentation section). The diversification of motivations affecting firms' usage of trade credit justifies further analysis by firm type for a select group of European countries (see Segmentation by Firm Type section). Last, a multidimensional analysis simultaneously examines geographical, sectorial, and firm-type categories in the usage of trade credit (see Synthesis: Multidimensional Segmentation section). Conclusions section concludes the chapter.

Trade Credit around the World

One way to develop interfirm relationships is through trade credit, that is, client's delaying payment for goods purchased from and services provided by vendors in well-established trade relationships. Motivations for using trade credit are multifaceted (see Chapter 2); it is therefore a persistent and global phenomenon in financial transactions. Growing firms invest in trade credit to develop interfirm relationships (Summers and Wilson 2003) in both domestic and international trade. A moderately in-depth analysis of trade credit must be conducted at the global level because national standards in collecting data are not homogeneous and the need for greater improvements in this area has also been expressed at the international level (Development Working Group 2011).

The degree to which trade credit supports international trade has been extensively discussed and has garnered distinct attention, particularly since the 2008 global financial crisis, as characterized by a correlated drop in trade finance and trade at the peak of the global downturn (Asmundson et al. 2011), showing that shortages of trade credit and trade finance services can affect international trade growth (International Chamber of Commerce, or ICC 2016). The measurement of such gaps, however, has been difficult due to definition issues. Trade finance assumes various financial obligations, with different degrees of risk mitigation and lending involved in facilitating the movement of merchandise between importer and exporter and vice versa (Baft-Ifsa 2011). Therefore, it encompasses both traditional bank-intermediated financial instruments and direct interfirm loans (Amiti and Weinstein 2011).

Recent estimates show that more than the half of the volume of international trade finance is supported by trade credit, and bank-intermediated trade finance services support 20 to 40 percent of international trade (Committee on the Global Financial System 2014). In light of relevant changes in time series on trade credit published by the Task Force on Finance Statistics (TFFS 2016), a reliable estimation of trade credit in international trade has used data on short-term trade credit insurance[1]

---

[1] The Berne Union's members represent over 11 percent of such business and, following integration with the Prague Club, the represented countries stand for 90 percent of the world's population (Berne Union 2016).

provided by Bern Union (Auboin and Engemann 2014). Specifically, the Berne Union collects quarterly data on short-term credit limits[2] by destination country. Therefore, the ratio of the credit limit to the amount of imported goods and services provided by the World Trade Organization indicates the importance of the extension of trade credit to international trade for a given country. At the global level, trade credit accounted for an average of 22 percent of international trade during the past decade, with modest variability since the global financial crisis and a current upward trend (ICC 2016). The patterns of the different geographical areas are correlated with global patterns, even though Europe and Central Asia, the Middle East and North Africa, and Latin America and the Caribbean appear to rely more on trade credit in international transactions compared with other geographical areas (Figure 1.1). In particular, Western Europe plays a leading role in trade finance markets, whereas China does not, and, at lesser levels, North America's contribution to international trade credit has recently started to grow again (ICC 2016). Among the reasons for the increase in the value of trade finance, financiers predominantly point out the increase of trade activities (International Monetary Fund, or IMF, and Baft-Ifsta 2011).

Income analysis shows that higher-income countries rely more on trade credit in international trade compared with middle- and low-income countries, even though all groups show growing reliance since the drop during the global financial crisis, with remarkable acceleration in the first quarters of the previous year in the analyzed timeframe (Figure 1.2). Consistent with the increase in the importance of the role of trade finance in facilitating activities in emerging Asian countries (IMF and Baft-Ifsta 2010) and supporting poor trade (ICC 2016), recent years show low- and lower-middle income groups overtaking the upper-middle income group (ICC 2016). Therefore, trade credit contributes to development.

The role of trade credit is crucial in supporting international trade, but it is even more important in supporting domestic transactions as has

---

[2]Financial intermediaries can mitigate the risk of nonpayment by other firms, and short-term insured trade credit can thus encompass insurance on bank-intermediated trade finance.

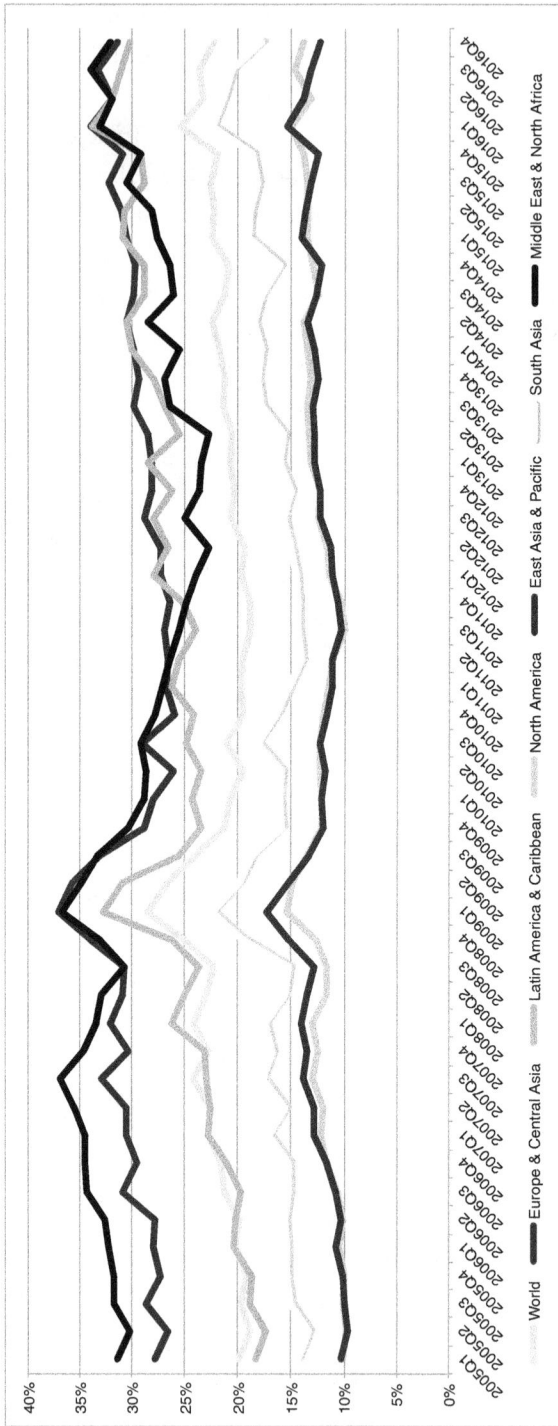

Figure 1.1 Trade credit in international trade

Legend: World — Europe & Central Asia — Latin America & Caribbean — East Asia & Pacific — North America — Latin America & Caribbean — South Asia — Middle East & North Africa

Source: Data from the Berne Union, the World Bank, and the World Trade Organization processed by the author.

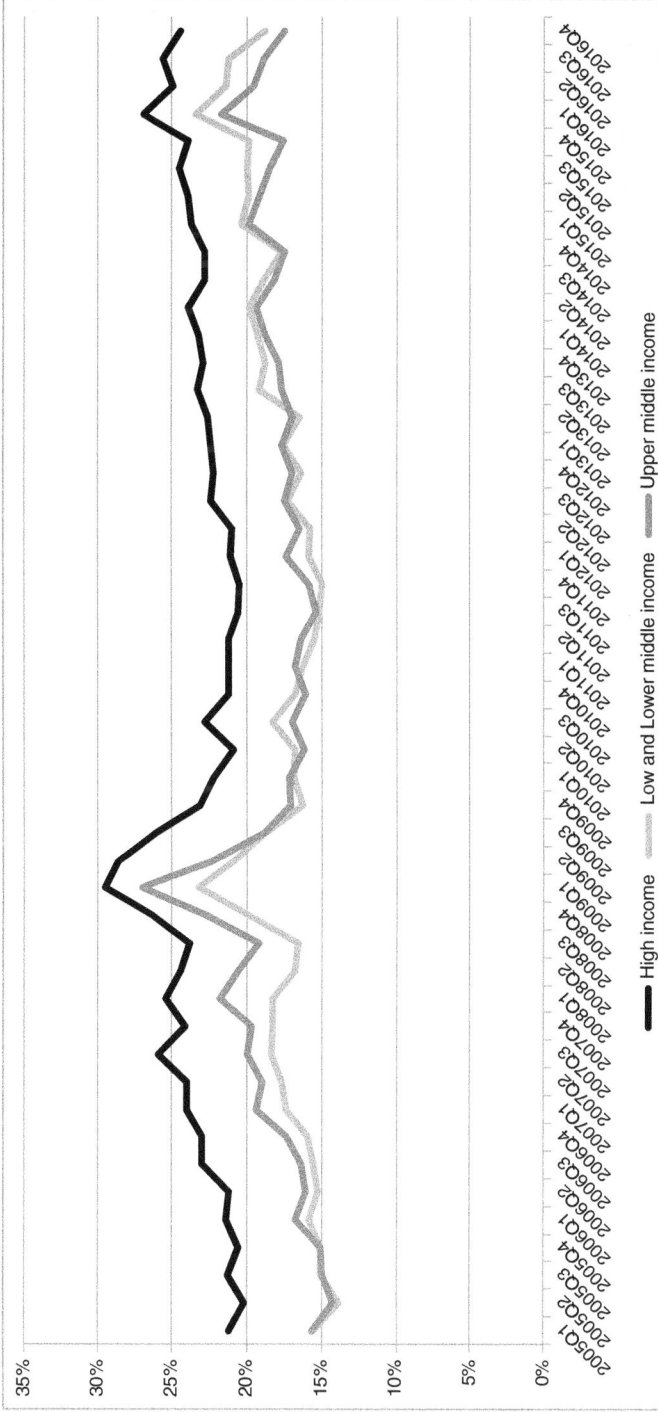

Figure 1.2 *Trade credit in international trade and country income levels*

Source: Data from the Berne Union, the World Bank, and the World Trade Organization, processed by the author.

5

been happening in developed countries. Trade credit ranks among the most important sources in the financial structure of firms in G7 countries (Rajan and Zingales 1995; Fitzpatrick and Lien 2013), and a positive net trade credit position supports investments (Beck et al. 2008), despite relevant variability both within and between countries (Seifert et al. 2013). Figure 1.3 shows the share of trade credit in total assets in the G7 countries between 2007 and 2015. European countries have a higher contribution of trade credit in total assets; moreover, the incidence of trade credit appears to be cyclical, even though it smoothens out after 2011. Anglo-Saxon countries and Japan are characterized by a modest share of trade credit in total assets, and, following the global financial crisis, the variability of the incidence rate appears moderate. Overall, Italy shows the highest contribution of trade credit to total assets and, with respect to other continental European countries, the gap is increasing over time.

A comparative analysis of year-end trade credit to yearly total sales (Figure 1.4) shows a moderately variable pattern for all G7 countries, even though changes in geographical rankings can be observed. Whereas Italy and France are first in terms of trade credit support to total sales, Canada and the United States rank above the other European countries. Notwithstanding the potential importance of year-end accounting transactions, the empirical findings can be interpreted in light of differences in the determinants of trade credit extension and the average duration of delayed payments (Petersen and Rajan 1997).

Industry Segmentation

Because suppliers lend inputs, trade credit origination and terms tend to vary by industry (Bukart and Ellingsen 2004). Therefore, the patterns are not necessarily clustered by geography. Moreover, even though the long-run averages of the share of trade credit in total assets are comparable across sectors, their variability is not.[3] In the manufacturing sector,

---

[3]Due to the unavailability of comparable segmented data, the analysis by sector excludes the United Kingdom.

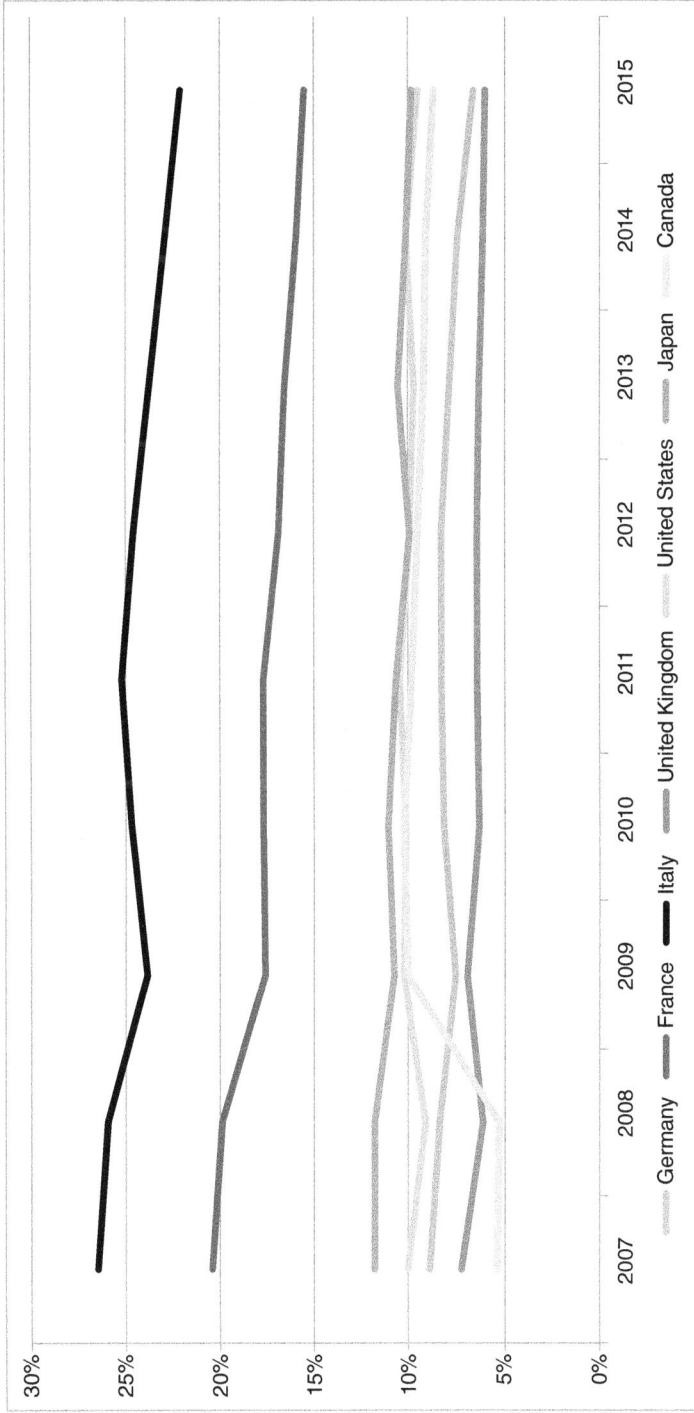

Figure 1.3 Trade credit in total assets in the G7 countries

Source: Data from Eurostat, Statistics Canada, the Statistics Bureau of Japan, the U.S. Census Bureau, processed by the author.

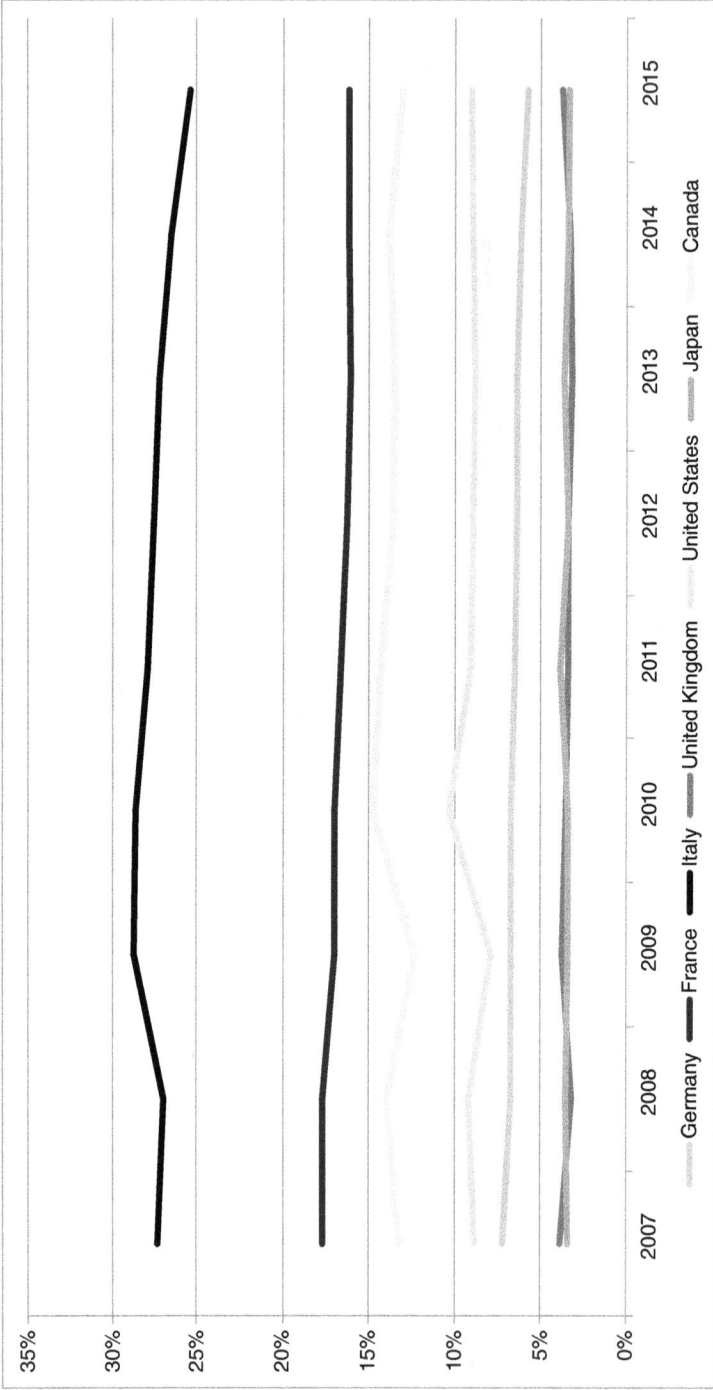

Figure 1.4 Trade credit in sales in the G7 countries

Source: Data from Eurostat, Bach, the Office of National Statistics, Statistics Canada, the Statistics Bureau of Japan, and the U.S. Census Bureau, processed by the author.

the contribution of trade credit to total assets is mainly decreasing, and, at the same time, the differences between countries are also decreasing over time (Figure 1.5). Although evidence for Italy and France is consistent with the aggregate data (Figure 1.3), Germany exhibits a relevant negative gap with respect to the other European countries, which can be explained by the shorter duration of trade credit extension (Atradius 2017). Japan is characterized by the most cyclical pattern, whereas the trade credit of Italian manufacturing firms represents roughly one-third of investments.

Compared with the manufacturing sector, trade credit shows remarkable differences between the wholesale and retail trade sectors (Figure 1.6). First, the trends among countries are not positively correlated; second, the ranking among countries alternates somewhat. Germany has the greatest relevance among the sample countries, whereas the evidence is exceptionally scant for Italy and characterized by an obvious cyclical pattern.

In the service sector, trade credit to total assets is greatest for Italy and lowest for Japan. Germany exhibits the strongest pattern of increase, particularly since the global financial crisis (Figure 1.7).

Analysis of trade credit turnover for the manufacturing sector (Figure 1.8) shows that, in Italy, sales benefit from the highest support, with the most delayed payments, even though the trend has been decreasing since 2011. On the contrary, support of trade credit in sales is the lowest for Germany and has hardly ever changed over time. Japan is characterized by a cyclical trend, whereas Canada, France, and the United States show an increasing trend in trade credit.

Overall, support of delayed payments for sales in the wholesale and retail trade sectors is the lowest among the industrial sectors, not exceeding 20 percent, even for Italy (Figure 1.9). In terms of trends, Japan's is cyclical, and Canada's is upward.

Overall, the service sector (Figure 1.10) in Italy contributes the most delayed payments to support sales, over 35 percent. Moreover, the gap between Italy and the second-ranked country, France, exceeds 15 percent, even though it is decreasing during the past years of the analyzed

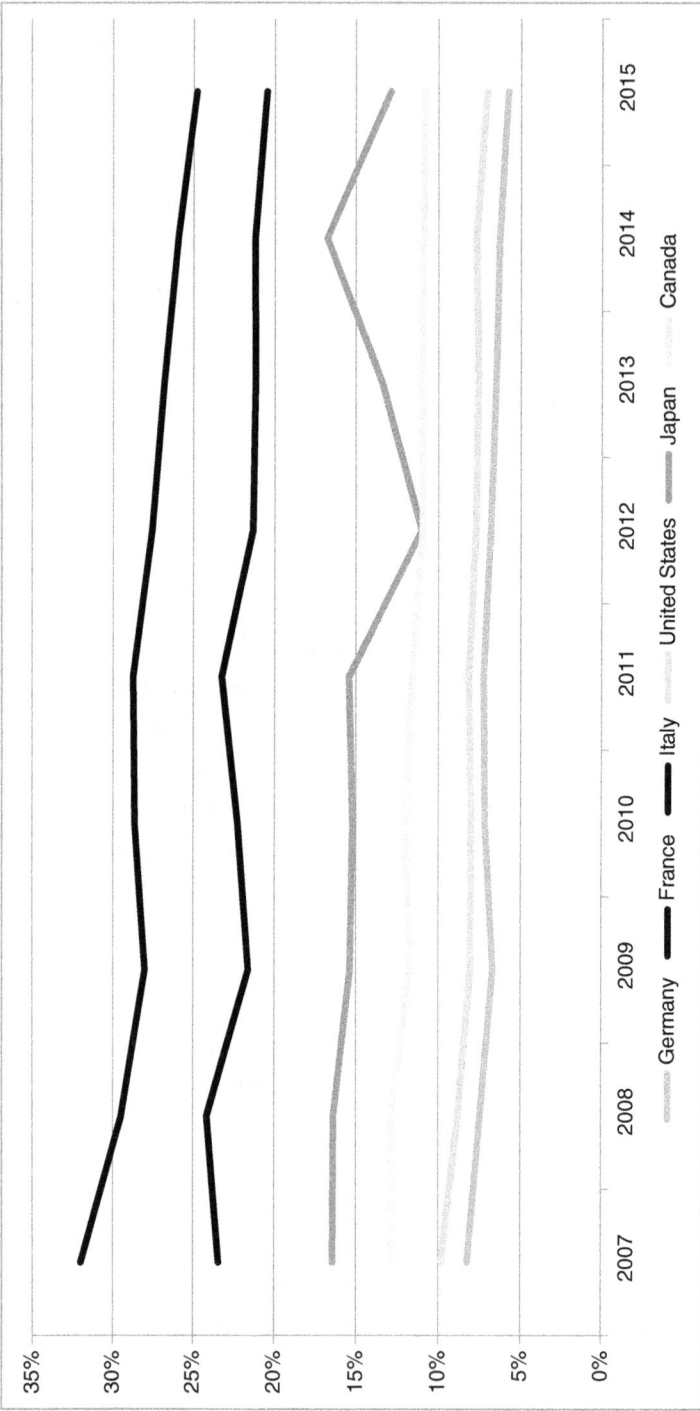

Figure 1.5 Trade credit to total assets in the manufacturing sector in the G7 countries

Source: Data from Bach, Statistics Canada, the Statistics Bureau of Japan, and the U.S. Census Bureau, processed by the author.

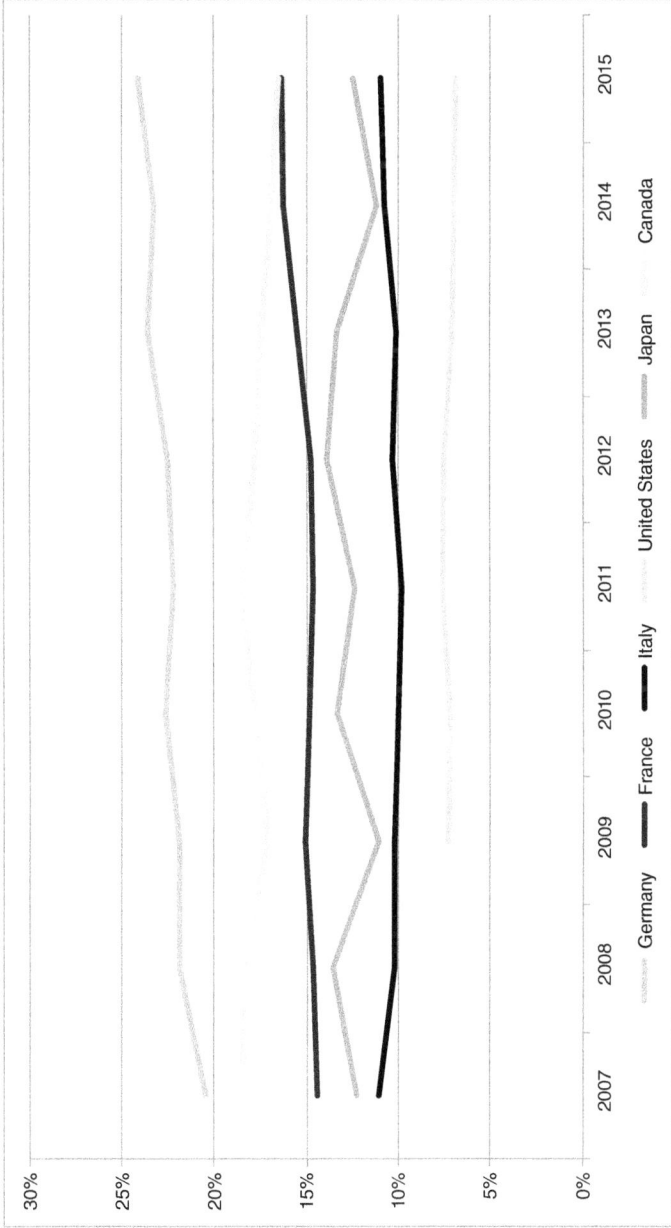

Figure 1.6 Trade credit to total assets in the wholesale and retail trade sectors in the G7 countries

Note: Data for the United States are available starting from 2009.

Source: Data from Bach, Statistics Canada, the Statistics Bureau of Japan, and the U.S. Census Bureau, processed by the author.

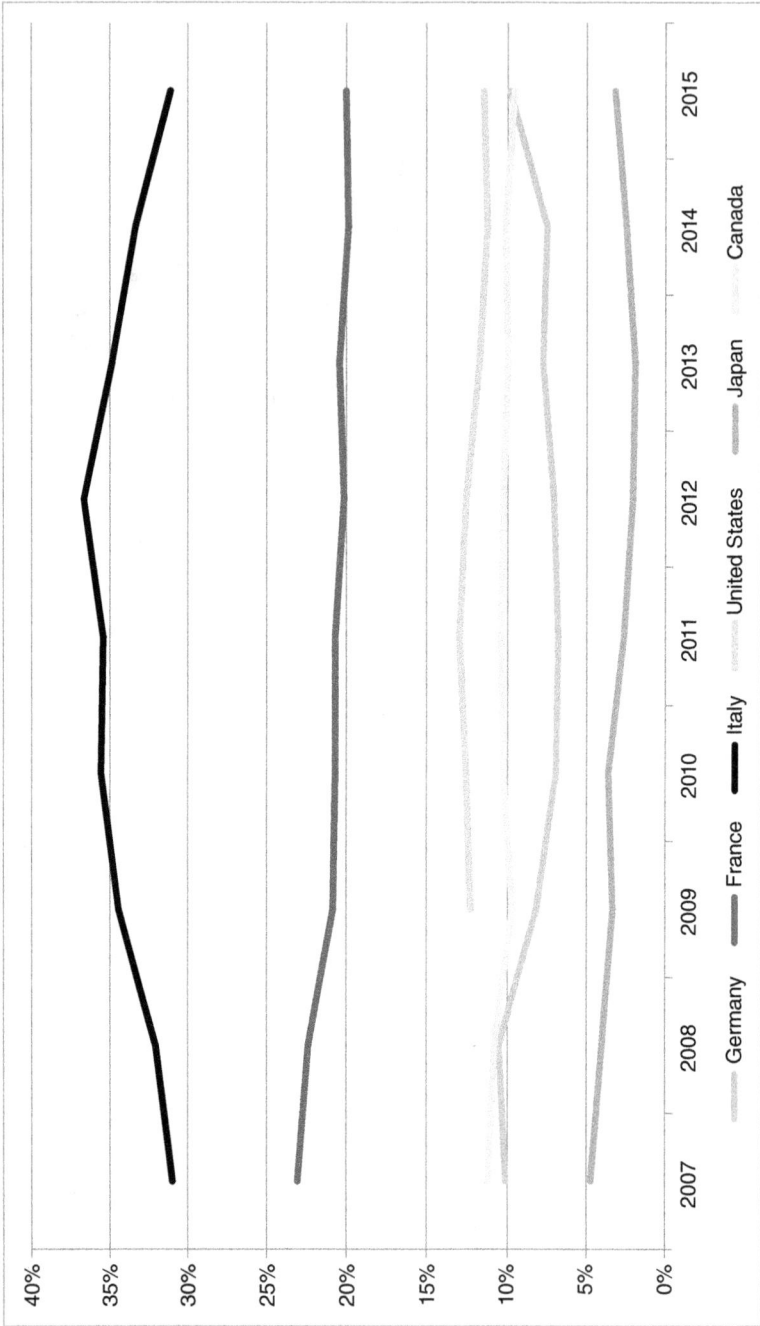

Figure 1.7 Trade credit in total assets in the service sector in the G7 countries

Note: Data for the United States are available starting from 2009.

Source: Data from Bach, Statistics Canada, the Statistics Bureau of Japan, and the U.S. Census Bureau, processed by the author.

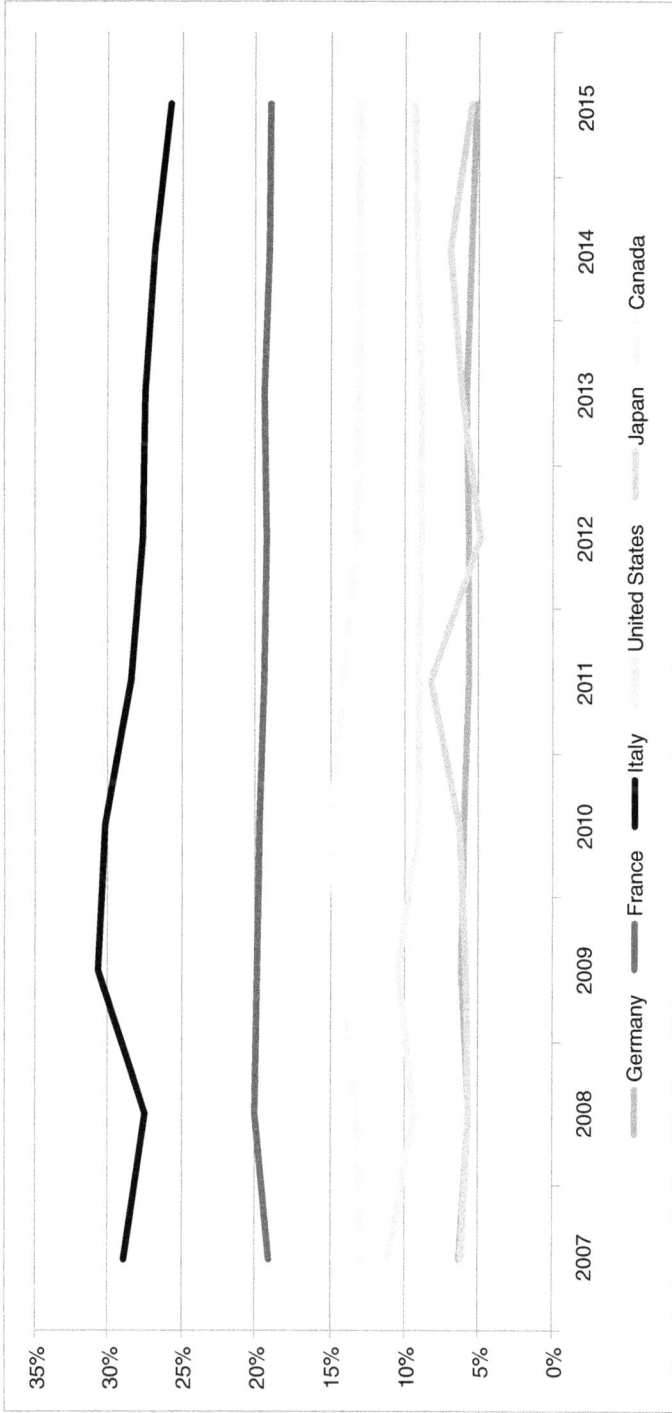

Figure 1.8 Trade credit in sales in the manufacturing sector in the G7 countries

Source: Data from Bach, Statistics Canada, the Statistics Bureau of Japan, and the U.S. Census Bureau, processed by the author.

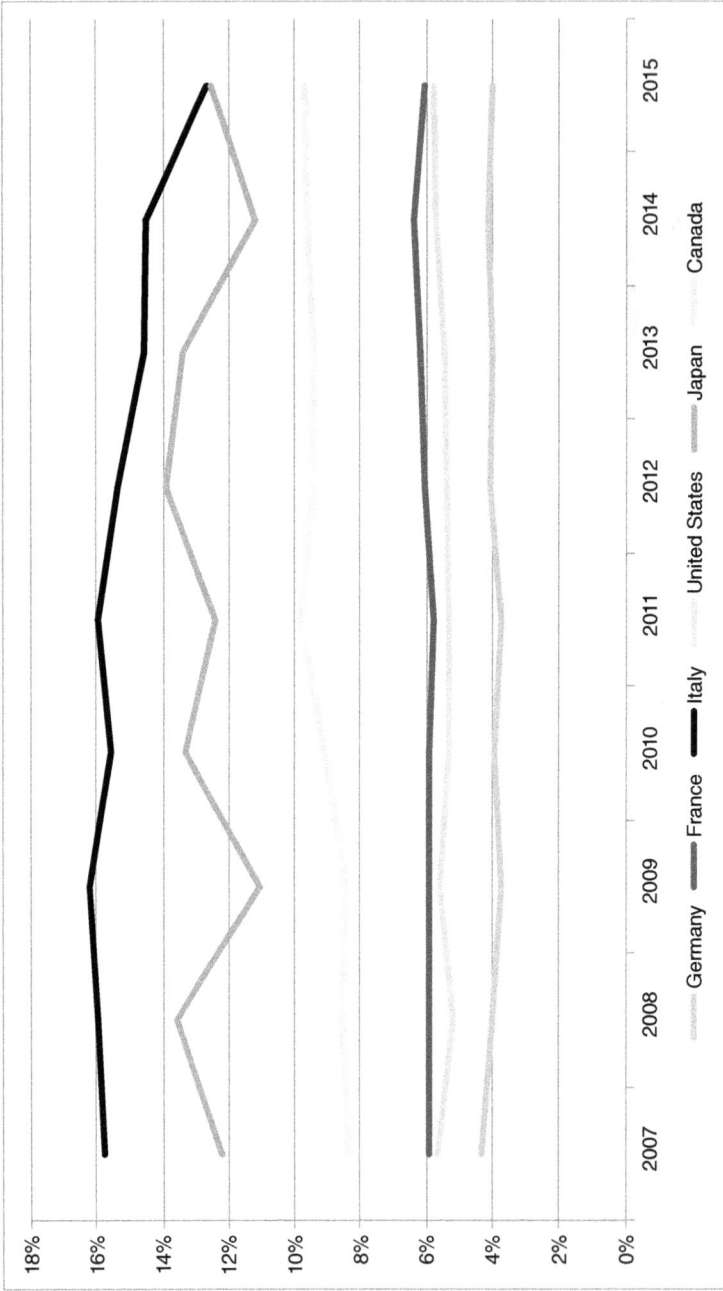

Figure 1.9 *Trade credit in sales in the wholesale and retail trade sector in the G7 countries*

Source: Data from Bach, Statistics Canada, the Statistics Bureau of Japan, and the U.S. Census Bureau, processed by the author.

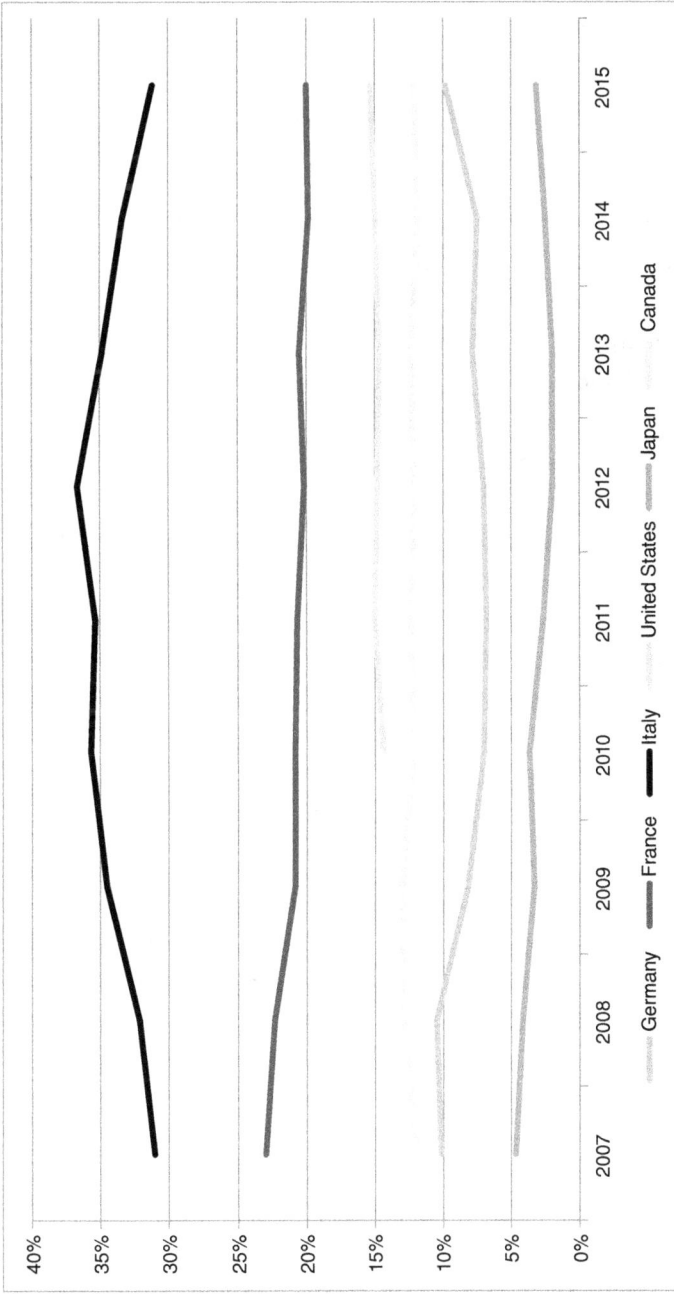

Figure 1.10 *Trade credit in sales in the service sector in the G7 countries*

Note: Data for the United States are available starting from 2009.

Source: Data from Bach, Statistics Canada, the Statistics Bureau of Japan, and the U.S. Census Bureau, processed by the author.

timeframe. France, Canada, and the United States are characterized by a stable trend, whereas Japan's and Germany's trends show modest growth for the previous years.

Segmentation by Firm Type

Cross-border analysis of the usage of trade credit by industry type has already shown that geographical proximity does not ensure similar dynamics. Inside a specific industry, the trade credit dynamics are affected by the type of firm. Available data for European small, medium-sized, and large enterprises[4] show that size can affect the contribution of trade credit. Overall, the trade credit for small firms appears somewhat rigid in the long run and shows a slight decrease for the past years (Figure 1.11). Within the time frame of analysis, since the global financial crisis, the gap between national patterns diminishes. The average gap between Italy and Germany exceeds 20 percent, with a much smaller gap between Italy and France.

Medium-sized firms exhibit the highest incidence of trade credit to total assets compared with firms of other sizes (Figure 1.12). Overall, the patterns of the relative gaps among countries are consistent with those of small firms: Even though France continues to rank second, the difference in the ratio of trade credit to total assets is characterized by a parallel downward shift. Therefore, medium-sized Italian firms have the highest proportion of trade credit to total assets.

A cyclical pattern of trade credit to total assets can be observed among large firms (Figure 1.13). Around the global financial crisis, a general reduction in trade credit is observed, especially for Italy and France. Overall, the ratio of trade credit to total assets for large firms is comparable with that of small firms for France and Germany and

---

[4]According to the Bach categorization methodology, size is defined as follows: small if the turnover is less than 10 million euros, medium if the turnover is equal to or greater than 10 million euros but less than 50 million euros, and large if the turnover is equal or greater than 50 million euros. See Bach, Methodology and Warnings, www.bach .banque-france.fr (6/1/2017).

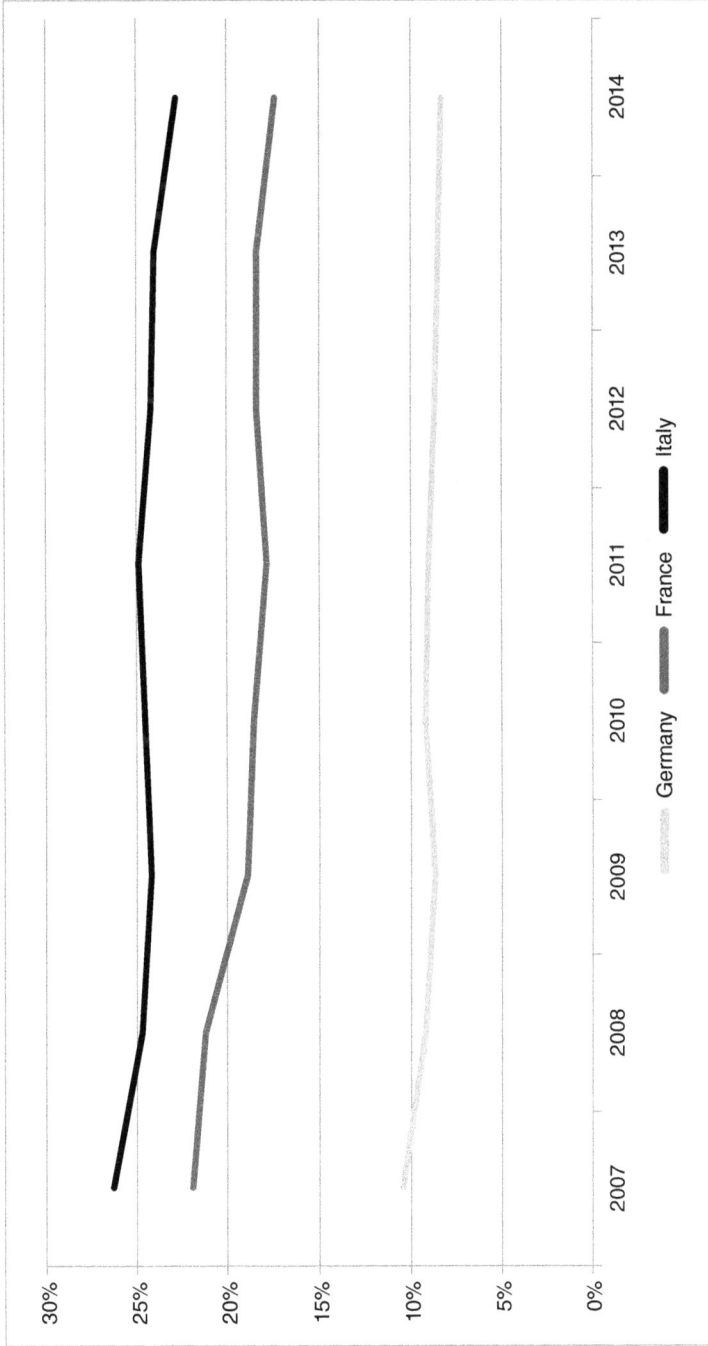

Figure 1.11 Trade credit in total assets for small firms

Source: Data from Bach, processed by the author.

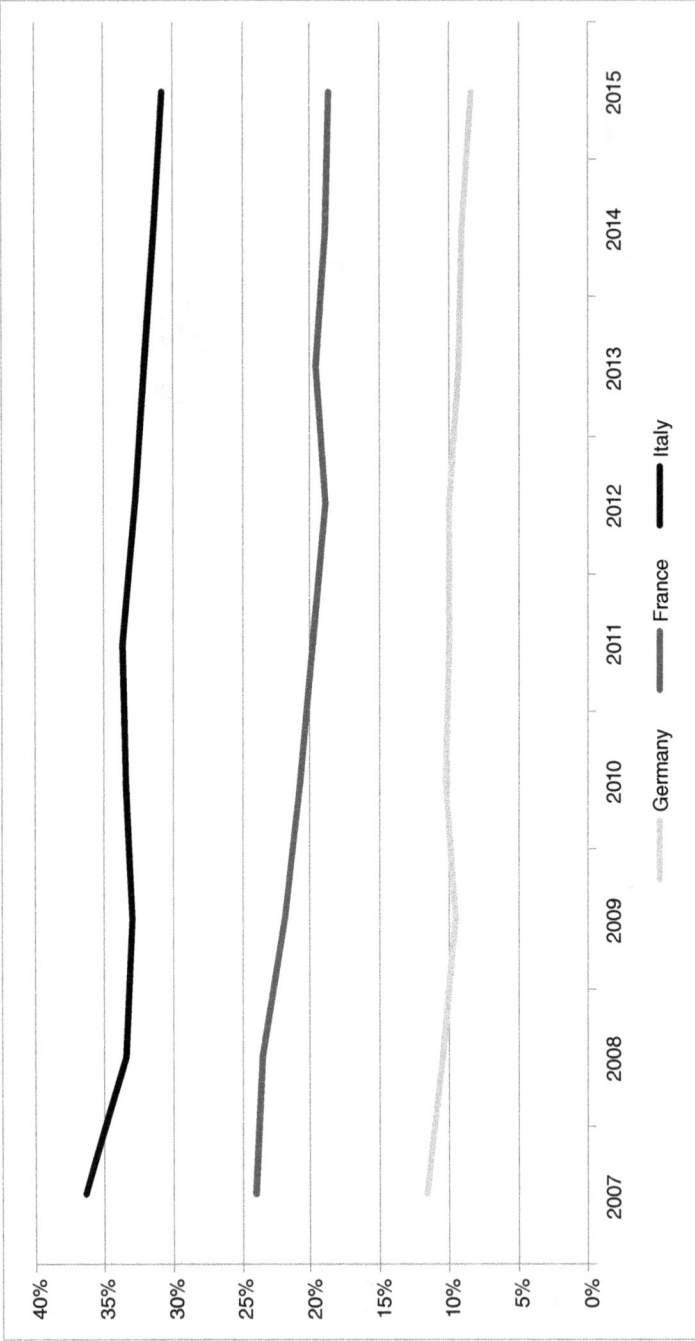

Figure 1.12 Trade credit in total assets for medium-sized firms

Source: Data from Bach, processed by the author.

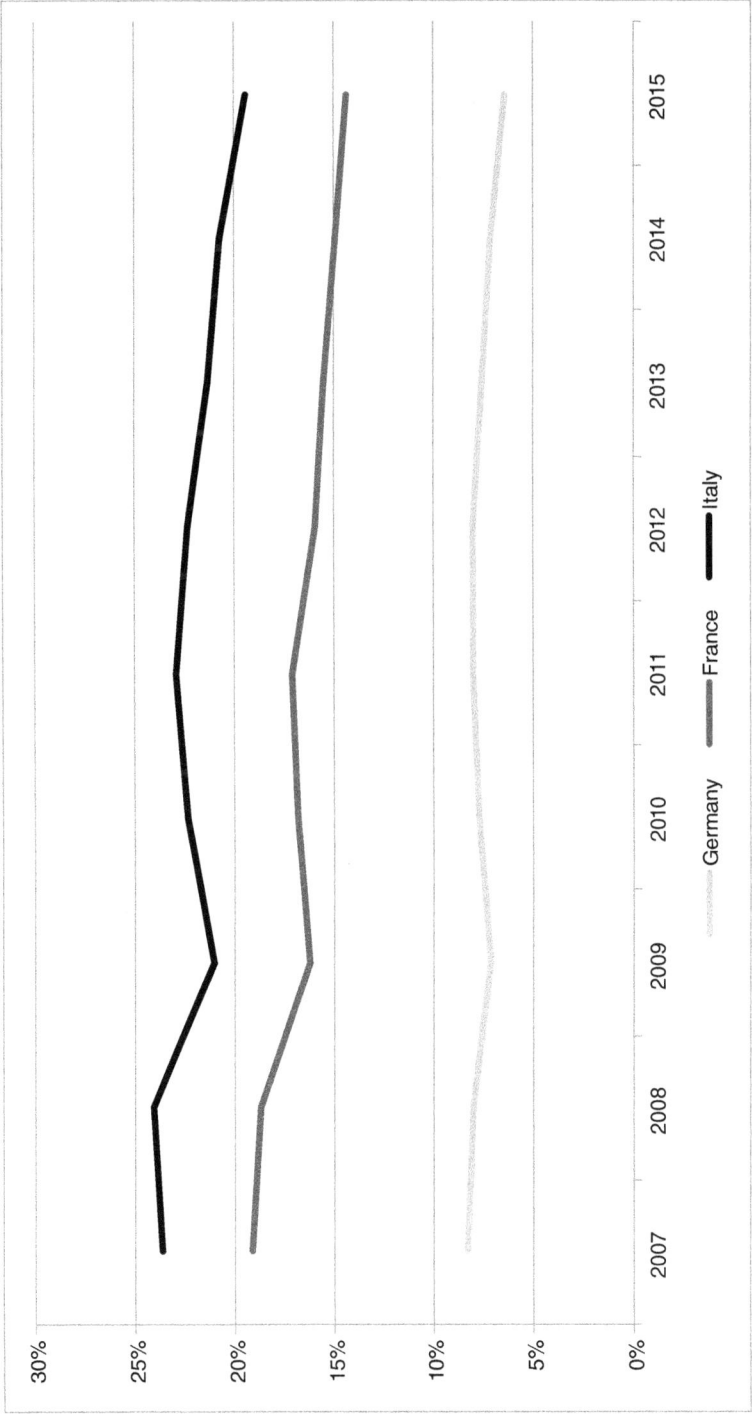

Figure 1.13 *Trade credit in total assets for large firms*

Source: Data from Bach, processed by the author.

larger in the case of medium-sized firms. National patterns, however, appear to be more correlated to each other than in the case of small firms.

An analysis of the support of delayed payments for sales shows a somewhat declining correlation between France and Germany (Figure 1.14). The more distinct pattern observed for Italy can be interpreted in light of the reduction of sales, particularly after 2008; nonetheless, the simultaneous decline of the ratio of trade credit to total assets prevents any increase in the average duration of encashment after 2013.

The support of trade credit to medium firms is comparable to the support of trade credit to small firms. Greater differences are observed for Italy, where, after an increase, a faster decrease has occurred, which can be explained by a rapid economic recovery characterized by lower incidence of trade credit.

The country affects the ability of trade credit to support sales to large firms. Whereas Germany has no detectable trend and France shows variability around 2008, Italy exhibits a growing trend correlated with that of other size categorizations (Figure 1.16).

Synthesis: Multidimensional Segmentation

The analysis in the previous section has shown that the usage of trade credit is affected by national, sectorial, and firm type characteristics; therefore, a synthesis can be obtained through a multidimensional approach.

Although Italy's top rank in the ratio of trade credit to total assets is confirmed, distinctive behaviors emerge. In the manufacturing sector, trade credit peaks between 2007 and 2009 for all the countries considered, consistent with the hypothesis that trade credit is positively associated with growth (Ferrando and Mulier 2013). The growth of trade credit to total assets is particularly relevant to small and medium-sized firms in all countries except Germany, whereas other countries are much more aligned with this aspect for large firms. Analysis of different countries

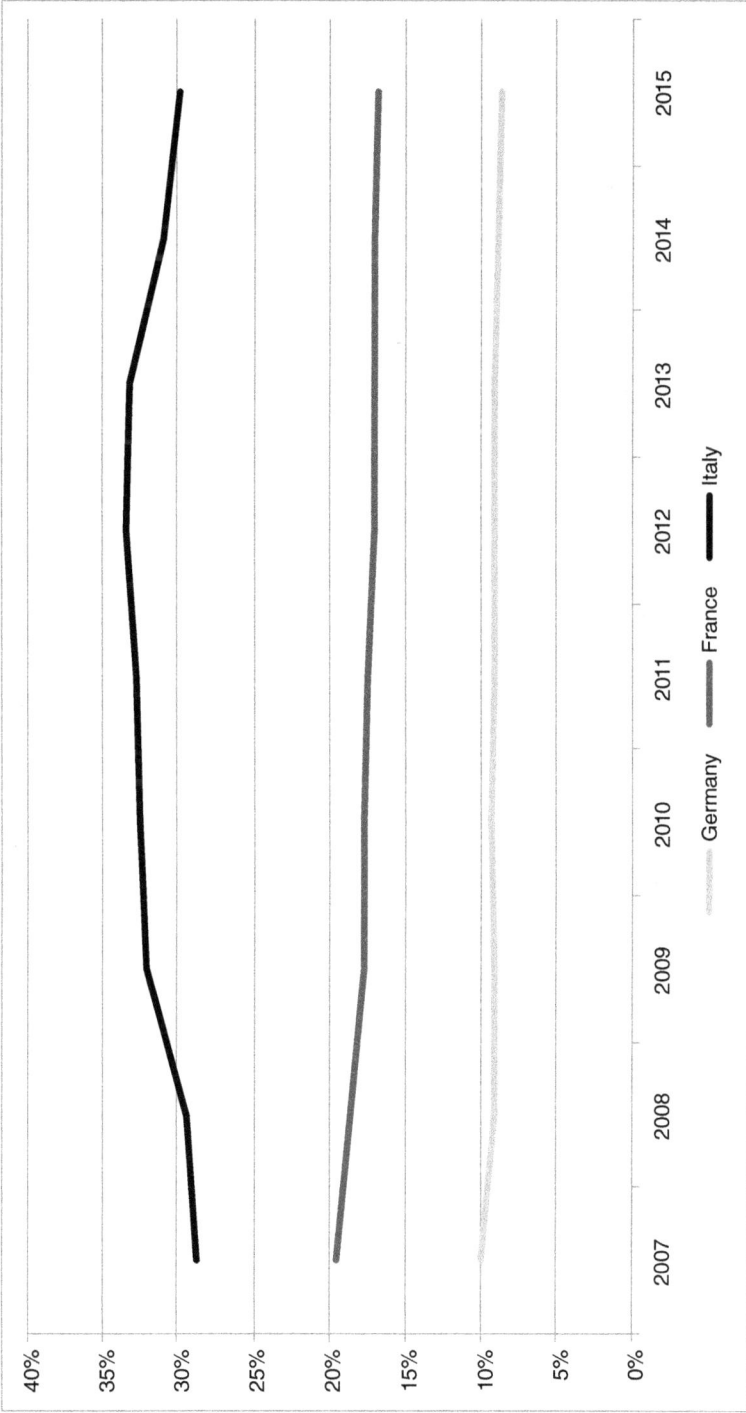

Figure 1.14 Trade credit in sales for small firms

Source: Data from Bach, processed by the author.

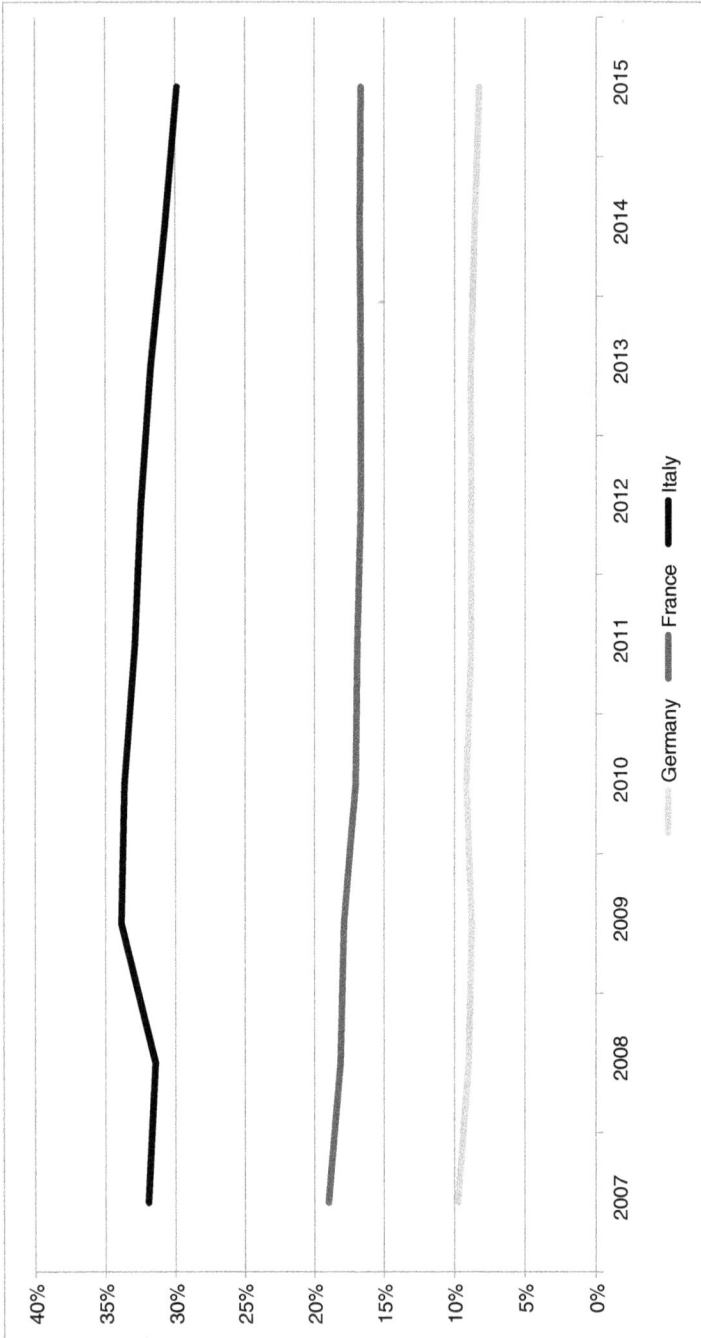

Figure 1.15 Trade credit in sales for medium-sized firms

Source: Data from Bach, processed by the author.

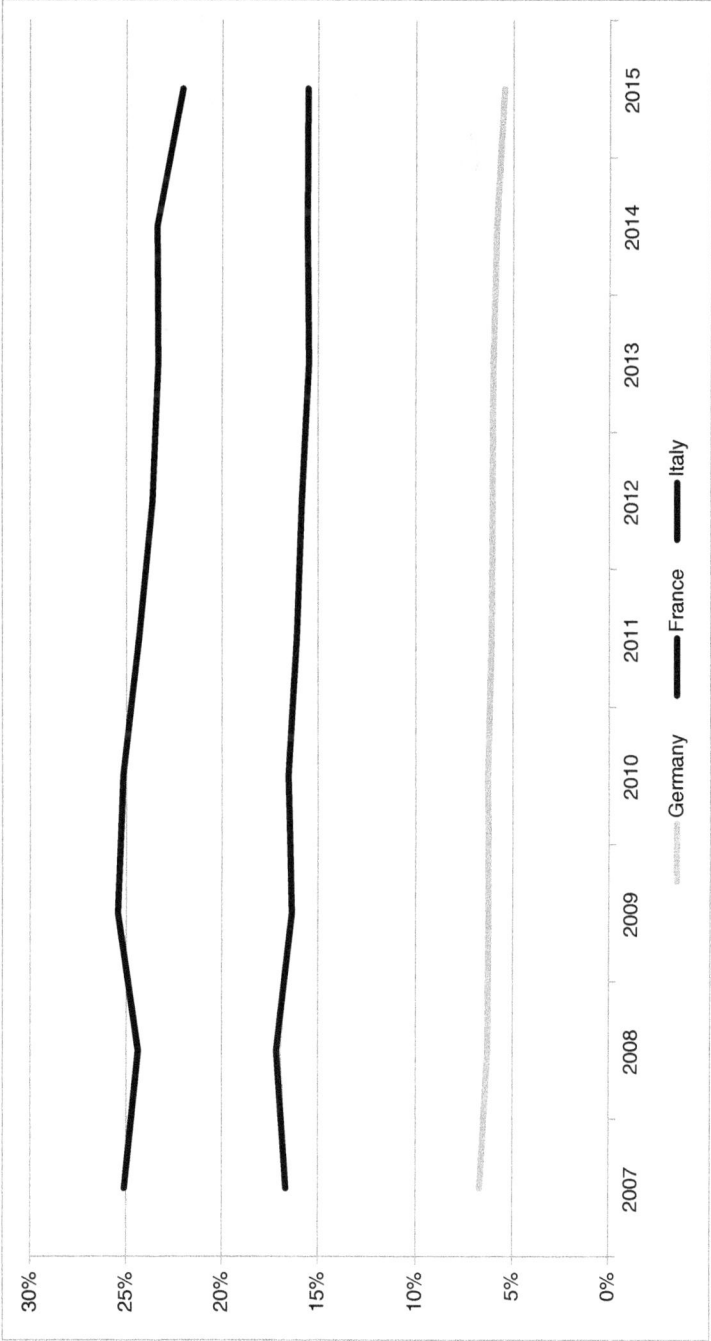

Figure 1.16 Trade credit in sales for large firms

Source: Data from Bach, processed by the author.

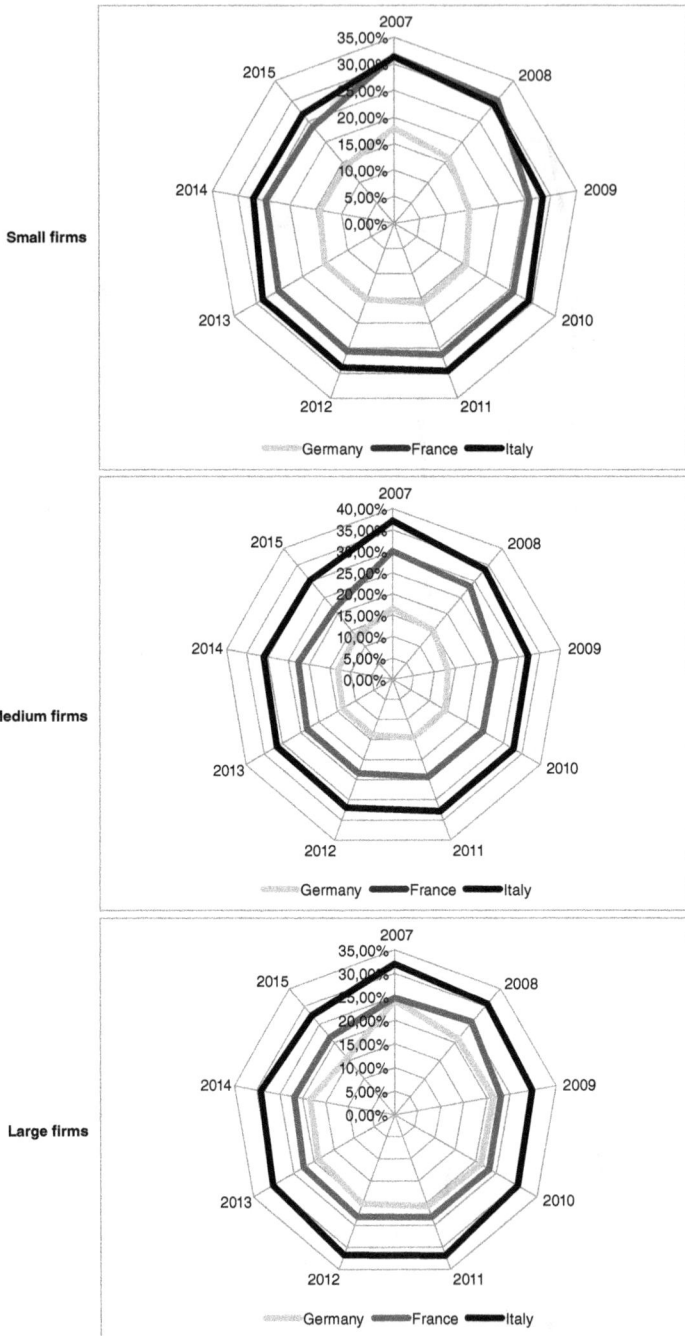

Figure 1.17 Trade credit in total assets in the manufacturing sector

Source: Data from Bach, processed by the author.

inside the dimensional clusters shows that small French firms are similar to small Italian firms, whereas large French firms are similar to large German firms.

Evidence for wholesale and retail trade (Figure 1.18) shows a weaker influence of the global financial crisis between 2007 and 2008 for small firms and an insignificant impact on medium-sized and large firms. The similarity between small French and Italian firms is confirmed, whereas medium-sized and large French and German firms appear largely similar, even though the variability of large German firms seems more pronounced.

The geographic variable is the most salient in the case of the service sector, with the distance between countries increasing with firm size (Figure 1.19). More specifically, trade credit exhibits a cyclical behavior for medium-sized and large firms in France and Germany, whereas a stable pattern prevails among firms in Italy.

The support of delayed payments for sales differs by sector, size, and country. In the manufacturing sector (Figure 1.20), although the relevance is comparable for small and medium-sized firms for all the sample countries, the support for large Italian and French firms is much greater than that for German firms. Moreover, the data show stability over time.

The support of delayed payments for sales in the wholesale and retail trade sectors is greater than in the manufacturing sector for small and medium-sized European firms (Figure 1.21). Nonetheless, a significant gap exists between countries, indirectly decreasing with firm size. In particular, the gaps separating Italy from France and Germany are some of the largest among various sectors for small and medium-sized firms. Last, modest variability arises only for small and medium-sized Italian firms.

The service sector shows intermediate levels of support for delayed payments for sales compared with other sectors (Figure 1.22). The trend appears stable for small firms, whereas medium-sized and large firms seem characterized by more obvious variability. Moreover, Germany has the highest ratio of trade credit to sales.

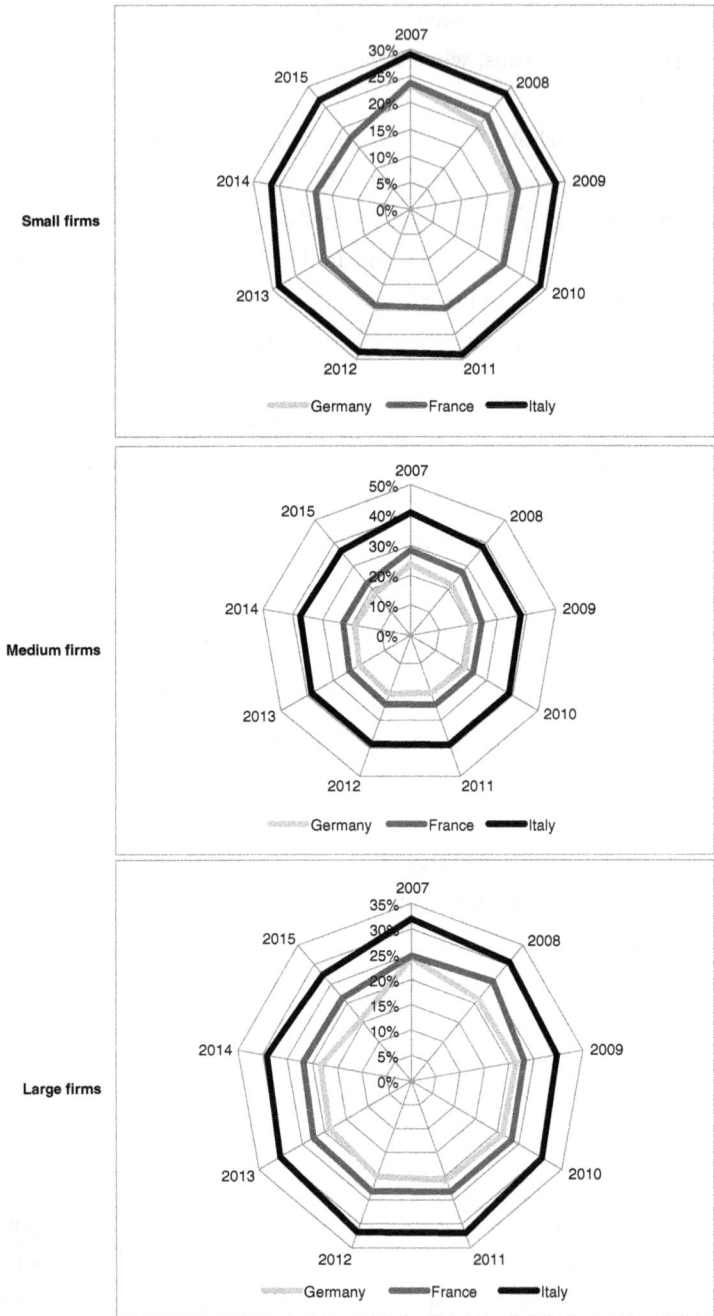

Figure 1.18 Trade credit in total assets in the wholesale and retail trade sectors

Source: Data from Bach, processed by the author.

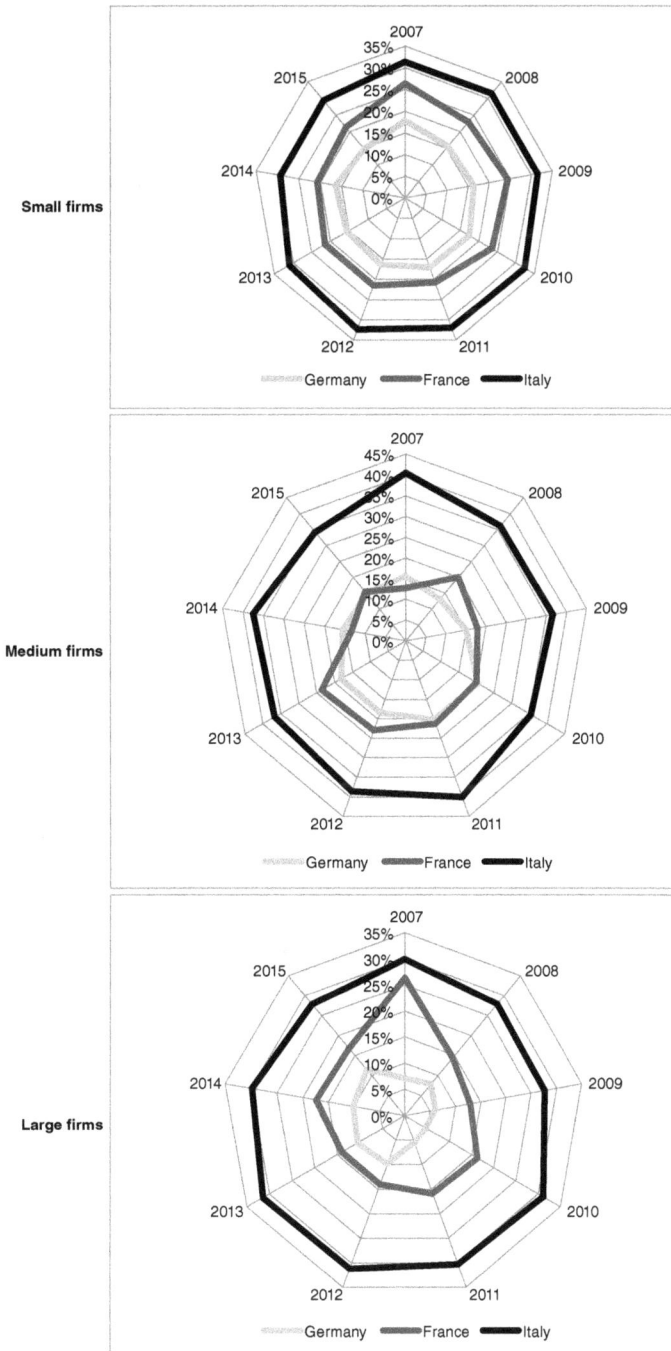

Figure 1.19 Trade credit in total assets in the service sector

Source: Data from Bach, processed by the author.

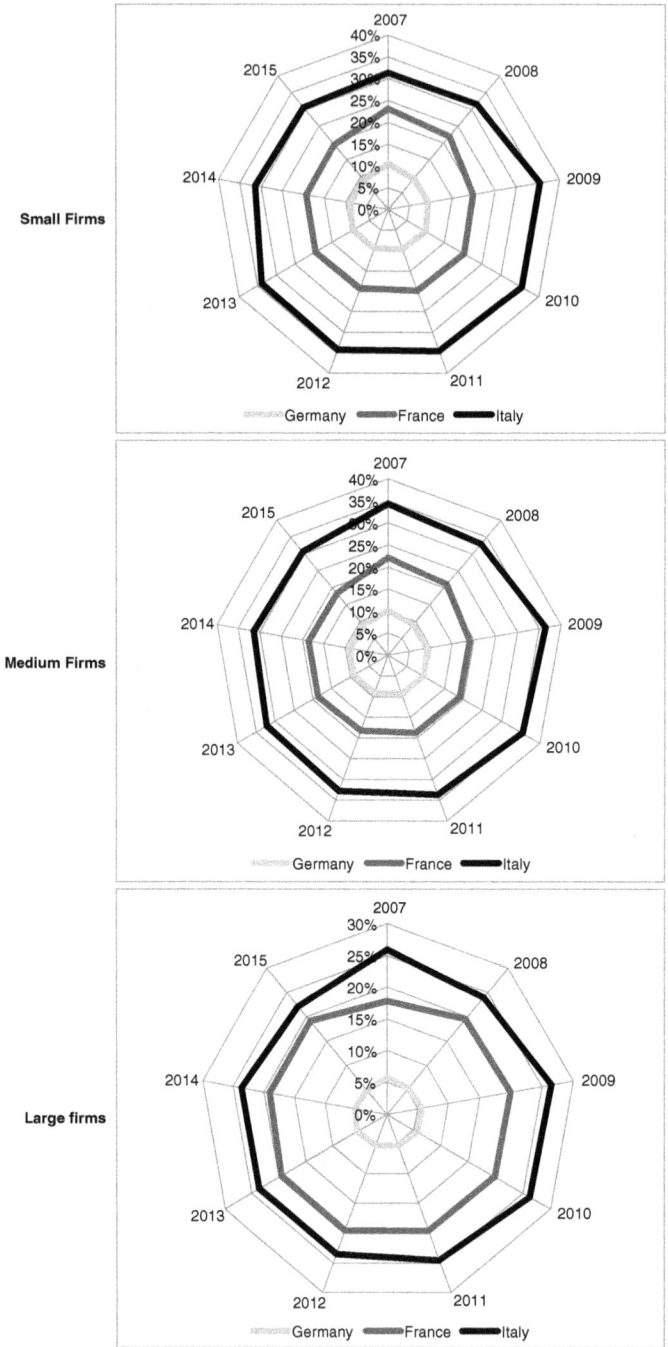

Figure 1.20 Trade credit in sales in the manufacturing sector

Source: Data from Bach, processed by the author.

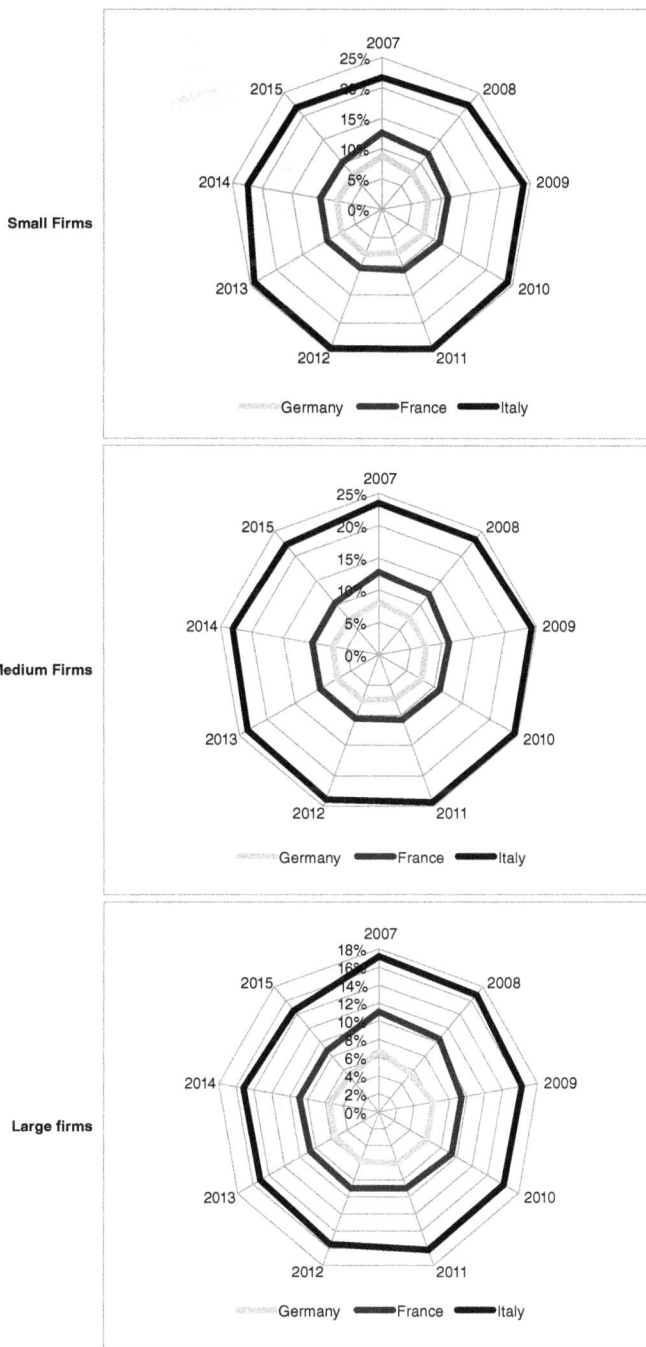

Figure 1.21 Trade credit in sales in the wholesale and retail trade sectors

Source: Data from Bach, processed by the author.

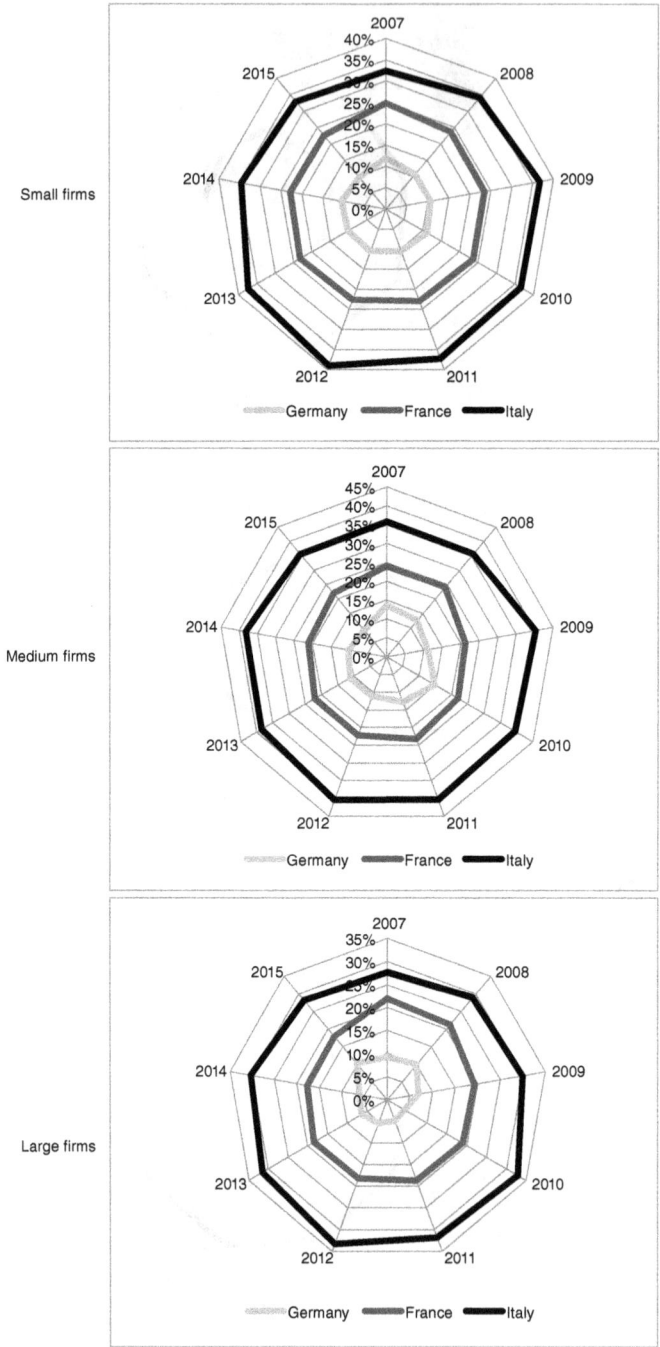

Figure 1.22 Trade credit in sales in the service sector

Source: Data from Bach, processed by the author.

Conclusions

Trade credit is used extensively in both international and domestic transactions. After a generalized reduction due to the global financial crisis, short-term credit insurance shows a current upward trend at the global level, driven by Europe and Central Asia. The role of trade credit in supporting development is confirmed by the growing relevance of trade credit in facilitating low- and lower-middle income countries in international trade. The relevance of trade credit in commercial transactions is even stronger for developed countries. After a cyclical pattern that emerged during the global financial crisis, individual patterns have emerged that exhibit greater stability and the ranking of countries appears unaffected over time. The incidence of trade credit to total assets is driven by European countries, with Italy ranked first, whereas Anglo-Saxon countries exhibit a weak incidence. Italy is again the country that most strongly supports trade credit for sales, but a distinction is also observed for some Anglo-Saxon countries. The analysis of aggregated industry and firm size data reveals greater differences than the analysis of geographic data. The manufacturing sector shows convergence of trade credit to total assets among the countries studied. Contrary to what was observed with other categorizations, the wholesale and retail trade sectors show Germany has the greatest trade credit to total assets, even though the terms applied appear very strict. Last, the service sector has the highest trade credit to total assets, even though support for sales is very limited. Segmentation by size shows that trade credit to total assets is greater for medium firms. The values for small and large firms appear comparable, even though small firms exhibit a somewhat rigid pattern and large firms' individual patterns are interrelated.

Finally, a multidimensional approach shows that the type of sector affects the influence of trade credit in total assets and in supporting sales. The extent of such an influence appears to vary depending on the country studied, even though this influence decreases corresponding to an increase in firm size. Larger firms are more comparable in terms of trade credit usage, whereas small and medium-sized firms' dynamics in trade credit usage are expected to be affected by local economic factors.

CHAPTER 2

Trade Credit: Theory and Empirical Evidence

Introduction

Trade credit is characterized by different business processes during a firm's life, from startup to maturity. Multiple theories and types of empirical evidence have been proposed to interpret this multifaceted phenomenon and explore its evolution in a changing business environment. It is therefore an active research area for academics and a key business driver for professionals. According to traditional theory, the supply and demand for trade credit are determined by economic sector characteristics (see Trade Credit across Economic Sectors section) and firm characteristics, with multiple motivations for recourse to trade credit (see Corporate Characteristics and Trade Credit Motivation section). Nonetheless, the broad variations in trade credit usage across sectors and types of firms have revealed the relevance of other factors in the examination of this easily adaptable balance sheet item. Trade credit plays a distinctive role in facilitating business relationships among firms by maximizing order quantities, with a positive impact on the profit of individual firms and the entire supply chain (see The Role of Trade Credit in Coordinating Business Relationships section). In particular, in developing countries, where financial resources can be limited, the opportunity to grow through increased business transactions can be financed through the support of supplier financing built on trust developed through repeated interactions, with a potentially positive impact on profits (see Trade Credit and Economic Development section). Under extraordinary conditions, such as during financial crises, the relationship between the usage of trade credit and other financial sources and also trade credit relationships can amplify the occurrence of shocks at both the inter- and intra-sectorial levels (see Trade Credit during the Financial Crises section). Concluding remarks are presented in Conclusions section.

Trade Credit across Economic Sectors

Trade credit allows firms to separate the delivery of goods/services in time from the payment of their price, so that the buyer gets more time to verify the quality of the goods supplied (Long et al. 1993). The inspection depends on the economic sector in question, as well as the innovation, complexity, customization, and perishability of the supplied good. Therefore, both the terms (Ng et al. 1999) and volume (Giannetti et al. 2011) of trade credit available vary according to the type of product and service sold and rendered. Given the economic sector and product type (Lee and Stowe 1993), buyers consider discounts for cash payments as signals of low quality in supply that is inversely correlated with the duration of production cycle. This is because the more time necessary to obtain the final product, the higher the perceived quality standard of the output. Therefore, firms making relationship-specific investments through research and development expenses offer more trade credit when selling differentiated goods, compared with firms selling standardized goods.

Trade credit represents a commitment mechanism when there is uncertainty about the quality of a product that can only be appraised after the product is consumed (Dass et al. 2015). Nonetheless, economic sectors are characterized by different levels of risk in light of buyers' demand characteristics: Intermediate products differ based on the probability of a new substitute product being introduced and consumer tastes that can differ in terms of capriciousness and ease of adaptation to new product's style and design (Chung 1990). Regarding contract enforcement, the type of product also affects the buyer's opportunistic behavior: Services and tailor-made products are exposed to a lower risk of diversion (Burkart and Ellingsen 2004). Moreover, in the event of trade debtor default, the creditor can start the recovery procedure, with the goods representing the collateral that the trade creditor can seize. Therefore, the economic sector also affects trade credit offers via the expected residual value of the goods at the end of the repossession process. In the legal context, the repossession process can be initiated by the buyer or a third party who may also have claims on the buyer's assets, such as banks and employees (Garvin 1996). Compared with financial intermediaries, suppliers benefit from a liquidation advantage on the repossessed good (Frank and Maksimovic 2004): Sellers are in the industry and can therefore recoup more value in the event of a trade debtor's default, with a positive mitigating effect on credit loss. Therefore, the type of good affects the risk mitigation of trade credit, and firms whose inputs are highly liquid (e.g., standardized inputs) or have high collateral value (e.g., differentiated inputs) are more likely to use trade credit (Fabbri and Menichini 2010).

Corporate Characteristics and Trade Credit Motivation

In economic sectors, trade credit is the output of the management of interfirm relationships. Therefore, there are several reasons for the use of trade credit. At the corporate level (Omiccioli 2005), the choice to use trade credit in interfirm relationships can be strongly motivated by support of the demand, commonly referred to as the real motivation to use trade credit. At the same time, financial motivations (Lewellen et al. 1980) affect the choice of trade credit to finance the purchase of the good, according to a substituting or complementary relationship with other financial sources. More recently, the role of culture has been discussed in explaining such motivations (El Ghoul and Zheng 2016).

Real Motivations

Real motivations imply that an offer of trade credit is an instrument to support market expansion. Consequently, offers of trade credit allow firms to separate the delivery of goods/services from the payment of the price, so that the buyer benefits from an extended period to verify the quality and accuracy of the order (Long et al. 1993). On the demand side, buyers consider discounts for cash payments as signals of low-quality supply, since the seller cannot allow the counterparties to verify the quality before the delivery of the product or the provision of the service is executed. In interfirm relationships, the buyer considers the opportunity to verify the supply a crucial feature, so that the extension of trade credit is a more effective solution than setting minimum quality guarantees in transactions, particularly in countries characterized by high uncertainty avoidance (El Ghoul and Zheng 2016). In particular, sellers are reluctant to underwrite legal obligations for disputes about the supply quality or quantity due to customer misinterpretation in the case of ex ante payments (Faith and Tollison 1981). Moreover, product warranties extended by new firms can suffer a low reputation among well-established buyers due to the higher risk of bankruptcy (Mateut 2014).

To support sales, suppliers can also use trade credit to avoid price discrimination between cash and delayed payments with two-part terms (Ng et al. 1999): The buyer can either pay the full price at the end of the delay period or benefit from a discount for payment shortly after purchase. The most common pricing approaches for delayed payments in commercial transactions are net terms and two-part terms. According to the first pricing type, the seller extends to the buyer a net period starting from the date of the invoice or the month-end, typically corresponding to 30, 90, and 120 days of delay. The two-part term approach is more complex, offering a discount to buyers for payments received within a short period and net terms afterward. In light of these commercial transaction pricing approaches, trade credit can be viewed as an investment, in which case the delayed payment and price cannot be considered independent (Schwartz 1974); rather, they are substitutes, with no opportunity to develop an optimal trade credit policy (Lewellen et al. 1980), regardless of the type of pricing approach applied. Moreover, the combined supply of finance and goods allows trade creditors to modify the offer conditions without modifying the price (Schwartz and Whitcomb 1979). This non-price discrimination will be advantageous if the demand of cash buyers is more flexible than that of credit customers; therefore, it is a way to make the transaction more attractive in the case of spot payments as well (Brennan et al. 1988). Since non-price discrimination concerns the impact of the offer to credit customers, it must be evaluated in light of bad debt, whose effect on performance increases with the price of the product (Blazenko and Vandezande 2003). Last, such types of non-price discrimination realized through the offer of trade credit can affect the fiscal effects of trade credit. All other conditions being equal, suppliers with a high tax rate prefer to extend trade credit to buyers with a low tax rate, since most

OECD countries allow reimbursements of the value-added tax in the case of debtor default (Florentsen et al. 2003). The use of trade credit as an instrument of non-price discrimination is reported to be strongly affected by country and corporate characteristics: Generous cash discounts are found to have been introduced for price discrimination and the strengthening of supplier–buyer relationships in the United Kingdom, compared with the United States (Pike et al. 2005), as well in countries exhibiting high power distance (El Ghout and Zheng 2016).

In addition to non-price discrimination, suppliers can extend trade credit to stabilize demand at both the micro and macro levels. At the micro level, trade credit allows firms to implement protective action in non-salvageable investments in relationships with buyers when the acceptance of a high rate signals a debtor's high default risk (Smith 1987), particularly if the seller's investment is greater than that of the counterparty. Moreover, trade credit represents a financial response that, by relaxing payment terms, supports the transfer of inventory warehousing costs to buyers by promoting a push strategy (Emery 1987), partitioning inventory costs. The seller thus sustains the financial cost of trade credit extension, taking advantage of transferring the operative costs of inventory management to the more efficient buyer. In light of an inventory channel of trade credit, a trade-off between holding inventories and trade credit exists, decreasing with the size of the firm due to scale effects in the holding costs of inventories (Bougheas et al. 2009). On the other hand, firms experience a positive impact on inventory investment when the net level of trade credit hold increases (Guariglia and Mateut 2006), because they can finance it with trade debt, even if they are financially constrained. Last, trade credit suppliers offer trade credit to build long-lasting relationships with repeat purchasers (Summer and Wilson 2003), and the offer of delayed payments can be interpreted as an acquisition fee requested by new customers or to retain important customers (Summer and Wilson 2002). In turn, they benefit from the customer's inertia and payment performance due to the high costs of switching suppliers that characterize differentiated products and are rewarded with a premium for both liquidity and default risk (Cunât 2007), which can be insufficient to offset the creditor's risks when the payment duration is too prolonged (Barrot 2016). The difficulty of changing suppliers increases with financial distress: Current suppliers desiring to maintain their product market will grant more payment concessions to buyers (Huyghebaert 2006), whereas new suppliers will be reluctant to sell to distressed debtors, unless under fairly significant restrictions and higher costs, such as cash on delivery (Altman 1984).

To stabilize demand against macro-level factors, sellers who have accumulated cash extend trade credit to support sales when money is tight (Meltzer 1960), particularly by offering delayed payment plans to new customers. However, surprisingly, trade debtors are not limited to small firms but also include large unrated entities (Nielsen 2002). Such evidence indicates a trade credit channel; that is, constrained firms substitute financial sources with trade credit in response to rising external financing costs. For small and medium-sized firms, such a substitution in financial and trade debt becomes greater with greater size, growth, and investment in current assets, whereas small and medium-sized suppliers offer more trade credit when facing a decrease in sales (Teruel and Solano 2010). Consequently, the extension of trade credit creates, at the aggregate level, additional capacity to acquire goods directly from sellers by incurring debt that qualifies as a monetary substitute (Laffer 1970). With respect to the business cycle, accounts receivable lags at the upper turning point of the cycle and leads at the lowest turning point (Nadiri 1969). Moreover, the extension of trade credit is an optimal financial response to variable demand (Emery 1987), particularly relevant as a smoothing tool when demand is characterized by a seasonal trend (Paul and Wilson 2006): Changes in production, due to inventory adjustment, and in trade credit should follow the seasonal trend of the demand curve (Schiff and Lieber 1974).

Firms can use trade credit for transactional purposes in managing everyday operations. In this case, the counterparties can agree to delay payment for a few days to minimize financial flow variability due to the dynamics of receipts and payments and pertinent transaction costs (Ferris 1981).

Financial Motivation

Trade debt allows buyers to delay payment for input by more than a few days by allowing firms to pay after the revenues are realized

(Lewellen et al. 1980). Therefore, the use of trade debt can be determined by purely financial motivation to offset operations against demand variability (Emery 1984) and can serve as either a substitute for or a complement to other financial sources. Theories on the substitution effect indicate that, in the presence of market imperfections, suppliers' costs for financial sources are lower than those of buyers; in other words, suppliers have higher liquidity. Therefore, from a demand-side perspective, buyers can use trade debt as a substitute (Meltzer 1960) and residual source (Jaffee and Stiglitz 1990) when internally generated funds are limited (Teruel and Solano 2010) and bank credit is denied due to a weak balance sheet (Danielsson et al. 2004). In particular, small and medium-sized financially constrained firms are found to be susceptible to the offer of trade credit to finance capital expenditures rather than relying on bank credit (Carbo Valverde et al. 2016). Moreover, during monetary shortages, the credit channel creates a substitution effect for financially constrained firms (Atanasova 2007), regardless of their size (Nielsen 2002), even though the magnitude of the contribution of trade credit in smoothing the credit channel is greater for small and medium-sized firms (Mateut et al. 2006). Greater use of trade credit financing by financially distressed firms strongly deteriorates performance, by approximately one-third, because of the high cost of this source of debt (Molina and Preve 2012).

If access to external financial sources is linked to technological efficiency, compared with expected returns from investing in trade credit, the extent of the substitution between bank credit and trade credit becomes unstable over time because of the difference in the nature of sources (Breza and Liberman 2017). This intensity exhibits a countercyclical pattern with respect to both lagged and coincident macroeconomic factors, such as the gross domestic product (Huang et al. 2011). Nonetheless, empirical evidence at the international level shows that trade credit is used by both financially constrained and unconstrained firms and increases in usage are not always associated with greater credit rationing. In any case, a relevant link between the usage of trade credit and the type of technology is observed (Fabbri and Menichini 2010). Moreover, the usage of trade debt signals to institutional lenders to increase lending offers when agency costs are high (Atanasova 2012).

Theories on the complementary usage of trade credit and financial debt have, therefore, been developed to explain why suppliers choose to utilize the services of financial intermediaries in their transactions (Demirguc-Kunt and Maksimovic 2001). Such theories stem from the competitive advantage based on the combined supply of finance and goods that allows firms to improve the operational efficiency of the counterparties to the transaction, compared to alternative financial sources (Mian and Smith 1992). First, suppliers benefit from a competitive advantage in the acquisition of information on a firm's creditworthiness (Berger and Udell 1998), which is particularly relevant in evaluating young and opaque firms. Second, suppliers benefit from continuous exchanges during the trade relationship that allow them to track a buyer's creditworthiness based on updated information (McMillan and Woodruff 1999) and develop soft information to characterize relationship lenders (Uchida et al. 2013). Moreover, because suppliers are engaged in the same nonfinancial transactions with customers, they can save costs in monitoring the business partner's revenues and thus add a second layer of financial intermediaries (Jain 2001). Third, if the debtor defaults, suppliers can easily recover the assets due to their knowledge of the supplied goods (Myers and Rajan 1998), and they can extract value from the collateral assets in a way that is not always easy for other creditors (Longhofer and Santos 2000). This advantage of trade credit suppliers over financial intermediaries is particularly relevant in common law countries (Frank and Maksimovic 2004), even if trade debtors experiencing debt reimbursement difficulties ask for renegotiation more frequently (Wilner 2000). On the other hand, trade creditors can have an advantage even in countries with less efficient enforcement and recovery procedures because they have recourse to informal guarantees based on self-defense mechanisms and conditional sale contracts (Santella 2005). From the supply-side perspective, the motivation for offering trade credit is determined by the signaling effect recognized by other financiers, based on the opportunity to share private information (Biais and Gollier 1997) that would be prohibitive to acquire (Berlin 2003). Empirical evidence shows that the extension of trade credit positively affects evaluation by other creditors and is associated with lower levels of collateral requirements and/or fewer commitments (Voordeckers and Steijvers 2006). Ex post, the positive impact of better access to external finance must be evaluated by trade creditors in light of empirical evidence showing a higher incidence of credit losses, as determined by corporate failure, compared with the banking sector, and relevance to creditor distress at the individual firm level (Jacobson and Von Schevdin 2015).

The Role of Trade Credit in Coordinating Business Relationships

It has been recently shown that the offer of trade credit is not limited to financially benefiting the supplier but that it also helps to overcome frictions between suppliers and customers (Breza and Lieberman 2017). Thus, the operational research literature has grown in volume by combining operational and financial decisions in supply chains (Seifert et al. 2013) targeted at optimizing the flow of goods, information, and financial flows across inter- and intra-company boundaries in the market (Lambert et al. 1998) in the face of market changes (Stevens 1989). Due to the complexity of supply chains, a challenging factor is the difficulty in understanding the coordination of the operations of individual supply chain members to improve system profits through incentives for decentralized decisions (Li and Wang 2007). In the long run, the coordination of the supply chain allows individual profits to increase at both the supplier and buyer levels (Abad and Jaggi 2003). Moreover, empirical evidence shows that such coordination affects the financial performance of the supply chain members (Yu 2013).

Among the different functions in supply chains, inventory management plays a crucial role in coordination due to demand uncertainty, leaving room for potential conflicts at the procurement and production interfaces: Suppliers foster stable volumes whereas manufacturers demand small quantities to limit the risk of holding inventories. To achieve coordination, effective supply chain mechanisms are implemented by supply chain contracts, information technology, and joint decisions (Arshinder and Deshmukh 2008). In supply chain contracts, the terms of trade range from preorder to consignment modes and the agreement adopted is frequently a combination of the two modes as the result of the coordination mechanism, which has a positive impact on the retailer's order size

(Cachon 2003). The optimal order size is affected by the extension of the trade credit period because the buyer can reduce the opportunity cost of the investment in inventories, compared with instantaneous payment (Jaber and Osman 2006). The supplier can alter the buyer's order size, benefiting from a reduction in setup, ordering, and inventory holding costs (Luo 2007), even for multiple heterogeneous buyers (Sarmah et al. 2008). Therefore, decisions by suppliers on trade credit extension are part of the supply chain. Depending on the terms agreed, inventory risk is borne by the supplier in the case of consignment terms or by the buyer in the case of preorder terms, which has a distinct impact on the efficiency of their own supply chains (Cachon 2004). Because it is preferable to avoid responsibility for inventory risk, a premium can induce the parties to share the risk (Ulku et al. 2007). Under financial constraints, the supplier will prefer to share inventory risk by preordering and financing it through internal capital and take recourse to external financing to raise short-term financing, regardless of retailer status (Lai et al. 2009). As an alternative to short-term financing, suppliers can finance a retailer's inventory through trade credit, which prevents exposure of the counterparties to default risk on financial obligations in light of demand variability when borrowing from a bank. By eliminating the hypothesis of free inventory financing in supply chains (Pfhol and Gomm 2009), trade credit contributes to increasing the efficiency of the overall supply chain. A risk-neutral supplier's combined offer of a wholesale price and an interest rate for delayed payments is unaffected by retailer status or the preordered quantity, so the retailer is able to pay lower interests and increase the size of the order (Kouvelis and Zhao 2012). The impact of the trade credit offer is particularly relevant to increasing the retailer's order size in the case of limited liability and financial constraint, while the supplier can prevent the retailer's overbearing behavior by discriminating trade prices (Cheng and Wang 2012).

Specifically, because asset-based lending reduces information distortion among the members in supply chain financing (Alan and Gaur 2012) and trade contracts are sufficiently flexible to overcome the limits of standard ones (Gan et al. 2004), risk-averse suppliers are able to coordinate financially constrained retailers' order quantity decisions only by both designing a markdown allowance and extending trade credit with a risk premium favorable to the retailer (Lee and Rhee 2011) for an uncon-strained credit period, as long as the supplier's cost of capital is lower than the buyer's (Du et al. 2013). Indeed, under a combination of markdown allowance and financial debt, the supply chain cannot be coordinated be-cause of positive financial costs that will limit the buyer from ordering the optimal size. To incentivize buyers to reveal the cost of capital to develop a communicative supply chain (Ha et al. 2017), uninformed suppliers can offer a menu of contracts: The higher the buyer's cost of capital, the higher the ordered quantity related to trade credit and the longer the payment terms, whereas high vendor costs are associated with limited quantities and shorter delayed payment terms (Luo and Zhang 2012). Once the cost of capital is revealed, a discount policy strictly connected with both the level of advanced payment and the order quantity can be evaluated to coordinate the supply chain with the retailer's default risk and stochastic final demand. When the retailer's cost of capital is high, the proposed mechanism will not coordinate the supply chain due to the high cost of advanced payments, whereas a higher retailer default risk will drive the supplier to limit the offered quantity that is far from being optimal and the proposed solution will thus be more attractive for coordinating the supply chain (Zhang et al. 2014). The relationship between advanced payment and a discount percentage can be affected by the supplier's expertise in re-covering distressed assets upon trade debtor default (Fabbri and Menichini 2010) and by the retailer's cash holdings (Bigelli and Sánchez-Vidal 2012) and market power (Klapper et al. 2012). In the context of multiple finan-cial sources, the retailer's inventory financing portfolio will be composed of trade credit, cash, and bank loans (Yang et al. 2016). In equilibrium, trade credit is always part of the retailer's financial choices, whereas bank loans play a residual role. Empirical evidence on investment financing source selection and value creation shows consistently that an increase in trade credit usage is associated with higher profitability and risk reduction and the strength of the relationship becomes greater with higher manage-rial incentives and entrenchment (Aktas et al. 2012) derived from divert-ing bank loans for private benefit (Bukart and Ellingsen 2004).

Even with greater coordination, market power along the supply chain can impact the goal of efficiency, affecting the distribution of enhanced total performance (Crook and Combs 2007). The focal companies of a supply chain, often very large and powerful, can impose their payment terms onto smaller companies, which in turn enforce their terms onto yet smaller companies (Summer and Wilson 2003). Powerful customers demand long payment terms from small suppliers even if they are not financially constrained, making vendors cut investment opportunities if they have limited access to external finance (Murfin and Njoroge 2015). To limit losses at the aggregate portfolio level, small suppliers offer discounts for cash payments to riskier customers (Klapper et al. 2012). Relationship-specific investments determine surplus in the interaction between the supplier and the customer that will be extracted by the counterparty with bargaining power. Powerful suppliers will, therefore, be less likely to offer trade credit (Dass et al. 2015) and will impose their need to resolve uncertainty on buyers through tighter payment terms (Pike et al. 2005), particularly when a small business entity is unable to develop indirect inter-enterprise relationships through associations or other networks (Han et al. 2012).

To smoothen the impact of market power on trade payment terms, a financial supply chain management approach can be adopted based on the optimized planning, management, and control of supply chain cash flows to facilitate efficient supply chain material flows and remove inefficiencies arising from capital constraints (Sugirin 2009). Financial supply chain management allows for addressing liquidity and working capital needs stemming from the supplier and buyer levels (Wuttke et al. 2013) and activating different routines based on the type of the firm (Howorth and Westhead 2003): Large buyers' suppliers can access pre- and post-shipment financial services with the aim of limiting overall supply chain disruption risks due to the inability of suppliers and, in turn, their suppliers, to deliver. In particular, post-shipment service allows one to minimize the costs of tied-up capital while maximizing the gains of received cash across all collaborating members through cooperative use of power (Hofman and Kotzab 2010). This will prevent members' shortage of liquidity from deteriorating under distress, which can have disruptive wealth effects for investors, particularly when intra-industry contagion is severe (Hertzel et al. 2008). Successful implementation of the financial supply chain can reduce cash flow risk, even though decision making requires proper evaluation of specific characteristics of the working capital of the buying firm compared with the working capital of the upstream firm. Geographical location and industry sector can determine different financial needs along the supply chain, particularly for the focus on buyers or suppliers (Sugirin 2009). Offers of financial supply chain services are based on the interactions between financial institutions and third-party service providers, providing business counterparties with solutions beyond the adaptation of payment terms. Financial supply chain services span from suppliers' and buyers' finance to supply chain financing solutions based on the interaction between financing and operational needs targeted at enhancing the efficiency of the supply chain (He et al. 2010). Through the use of reverse factoring, based on financial management services beyond the adaptation of payment terms (Seifert and Seifert 2007), supply chain finance frequently consists of an automated solution that enables buying firms to use reverse factoring with their entire supplier base. This means the suppliers are not selected based on specific factors, often providing flexibility and transparency to the payment process. In particular, supply chain finance has found successful application in the automotive sector and in global supply chains characterized by large buyers sourcing from Asian countries (Sugirin 2009).

Trade Credit and Economic Development

The development of financial markets is associated with growth. In countries with poor and concentrated financial institutions, firms can be hindered from accessing traditional markets (Beck et al. 2003). A possible solution to allocate funds to support firm growth is therefore supplier finance in the form of trade credit (Fisman and Love 2003), given the advantage in evaluating constrained firms stemming from business relationships (Petersen and Rajan 1997). Following the transition from a centrally planned economy to deregulation, firms are no longer allowed to obtain financial sources, regardless of creditworthiness; therefore, information asymmetries can be severe and make the cost of funds prohibitive. Because of the entrepreneurial self-help that characterizes evolution toward a market economy, private firms can have no bank credit but can still finance through trade due to the development of trust from repeated interactions (McMillan and Woodruff 2002).

Empirical evidence for Eastern European countries shows that the extension of bank credit was very concentrated at the beginning of the transition period in Poland and, therefore, financed private firms used to extend trade credit to constrained firms, driving the recovery of the economy (Coricelli 1996). Firms using trade credit are found to have greater success in obtaining bank loans because trade credit contributes to diminishing information costs. Therefore suppliers—and not banks—played a special role compared with other lenders in post-socialist Russia and complemented financial institutions' credit offers (Cook 1999).

Although much of formal finance in China has been targeted at state-owned entities, trade credit has not played a special role in sustaining China's extreme economic growth, compared with other forms of external finance (Cull et al. 2009). Most of the trade credit was extended by unprofitable state-owned entities to constrained private firms under a loan redistribution scenario allowing for substitution between bank credit and trade credit, while private firms offered trade credit only when high profitability levels were reached in order not to subtract resources from investments. With trade credit comprising informal finance sources in China, it appears to have affected the growth of small firms that require trade credit for financial motivation (Ge and Qiu 2007); in any case, it plays a co-funding role with respect to bank credit (Degryse et al. 2016). The use of interfirm finance is affected by substitutability for cash holdings. Accounts payable are associated with lower cash holdings, particularly after banks' offers of trade credit financing products were broadened, even though the substitution is far from perfect, showing that imperfections require Chinese firms to hold cash reserves to address payables (Wu et al. 2012).

In Indonesia, offers of trade credit are affected by the market structure (Hyndman and Serio 2010). The transition from a monopoly to a duopoly is associated with a strong jump in trade credit offers, and greater competition is associated with a weaker increase in interfirm finance and can decrease sharply after reaching a critical level. The motivation behind the observed pattern is a traditional competition effect, where the entry of new suppliers modifies the trade credit price but not the cash price and, therefore, only the proportion of credit sales will increase.

Trade credit is found to be a financial alternative for Mexican firms when bank loans and intragroup funding are not available. Moreover, the stability of the offer of trade credit allows firms to better plan investments in fixed assets (Messmacher 2001).

The availability of trade credit also impacts capacity utilization (Fisman 2001). Evidence from African countries shows that firms with access to trade credit have a lower probability of exposure to raw material stockouts and are consequently characterized by higher utilization of invested capital, particularly in inventory-intensive industries.

The wide utilization of trade credit in developing economies impacts firm profitability. By focusing on working capital, empirical evidence from Jordan small firms' performance shows that in a small economy it increases with the length of the cash conversion cycle; however, there is no significant evidence indicating that the reduction of the average duration of receivables is associated with higher value (Abuzayed 2012). On the contrary, empirical evidence for a large, fast-growing economy such as China, where financing path is not homogeneous among firms, shows an insignificant impact of trade credit on profitability (Li et al. 2016). Moreover, the substitution of letters of credit with open account payment in international trade has dramatically increased the relevance of foreign receivables to exporters' balance sheets. Therefore, exposure to debtor default has fostered a greater development of models used for predicting multilateral trade credit risks (Tang and Chi 2005).

More recently, literature has provided empirical evidence on the role of trade credit in supporting growth, even in developed countries. The fostering of value added is positively associated with the trade credit channel, whereas an inverse relationship holds true for bank credit (Ferrando and Mulier 2013). Tighter credit terms are found to depress trade volume, particularly for small suppliers (Breza and Liberman 2017), even though the outcomes of more strict agreements can be affected by the level of demand elasticity, since in more competitive markets that are characterized by inelastic demand a reduction in expected bankruptcy risk can foster the entry of newcomers (Barrot 2016). On the investment side, trade credit is found to limit financially constrained firms (Carbo Valverde et al. 2016) and the crowding-out by the offer of trade credit does not prevent overinvestment by managers but eliminates future growth opportunities (Murfin and Njoroge 2015).

Trade Credit during the Financial Crisis

Suppliers tend to assist customers in distress to maintain long-term relationships. Therefore, one can expect that, in response to the credit crunch characterizing financial crises, suppliers will support their clients by replacing the shortage of bank credit with an offer of trade credit. On the other hand, as a complementary source, trade credit can decrease with a bank credit crunch. Given the short-term nature of trade finance exposures, banks have been able to quickly reduce their exposures in times of stress. Therefore, trade finance could act as a stress conduit from the financial system to the real economy when banks run down trade finance books in response to funding and liquidity strains (Committee on the Global Financial System 2014). Given this perspective, one can see that the opportunity to substitute bank credit depends on the supplier's fundamentals, such as the size, financial position, and geographical diversification of the business activity affecting the firm's credit quality. Suppliers with a weak financial position before the crisis reduced their offer following a reduction in the bank's short-term debt offers. Evidence from the 1997 Asian crisis and 1994 peso devaluation shows that trade credit provided and received increased immediately after the crisis but the extension of trade credit subsequently collapsed, even more than sales did, and continued to decline for several years (Love et al. 2007). During financial crises, exporting firms are found to have less access to trade credit compared with non-exporters, and, therefore, frictions arise during financial crises (Coulibaly et al. 2013). Specifically, the East Asian countries' data for the year 1998 show that the contraction of trade credit extended to customers led to a shorter average duration of credit terms, higher costs for customers, and greater discounts for cash payments (Love and Zaidi 2010). Empirical evidence from the study of global financial crisis strongly contradicts the substitution hypothesis on trade credit and bank credit and reveals a procyclical impact of the complementary relationship, particularly for intermediate-risk firms (Munoz et al. 2016).

Given a network perspective of interfirm relationships, where firms borrow from and lend to each other because of a strict relationship between trade credit and debt choices (Gibilaro and Mattarocci 2010), the negative shock of liquidity at the individual level can force exposed entities to default on their suppliers (Kiyotaki and Moore 1997), activating chain defaults and amplifying idiosyncratic shocks. The impact can be particularly severe when firms' productions are not correlated (Direr 2001), which can be further exacerbated because of an aggregate shortage of liquidity that might occur during a supply-driven global financial crisis when alternative sources of financing are extensively used to compensate for the lack of available credit from banks and financial markets (Ivashina and Scharfstein 2010). Financially constrained customers are forced to cut capital expenditures (Carbo Valverde et al. 2016) and pass on their liquidity shock upstream, to their suppliers, allowing liquidity shocks to propagate along the supply chain in a way that depends on the heterogeneity of the units involved in the production network (Battiston et al. 2007). This is particularly the case for the increase in trade credit defaults of small and constrained firms as they run up against large firms acting as final providers of liquidity (Boissay and Gropp 2013) that can diminish the shock by relaxing the maturity period (Menichini 2011). During such shocks, the match between the demand for and offer of trade credit improves, but the positive relationship between the risk of insolvency and the demand for trade credit increases as well. Firms holding high levels of trade receivables postpone payments to their suppliers to avoid the increase in insolvency risk (Bastos and Pintado 2013). Only suppliers with precommitted credit lines are able to support the extension of trade credit during financial crises without affecting their own creditworthiness. Therefore, the use of trade credit by financially constrained firms is a function of the suppliers' liquidity as affected by the industry's dependence on external finance (Garcia-Appendini and Montoriol-Garriga 2013).

The propagation of shocks along the supply chain can follow a downward trend as well. Constrained suppliers can reduce the extension of trade credit because of liquidity problems stemming from the reduction of bank credit, which exhibits a strong positive causal relationship with account receivables during financial crises (Yang 2011), particularly for trade debtors in vulnerable financial positions (Tsuruta 2013). Moreover, in light of empirical evidence showing a positive relationship between trade credit usage and payment slowdowns, particularly for small domestic businesses (Mach 2014), suppliers tend to reduce the extension of trade credit to limit counterparty credit risk. This can affect the ongoing business of the firm, since the borrower is often a major customer. In the event of counterparty default, trade creditor's losses are determined by both the credit exposure in the balance sheet and the reduction of future earnings if the customer is not quickly replaced (Jorion and Zhang 2009). Empirical evidence shows that the suppliers and customers of firms of unique or specialized products are expected to be strongly affected by the distress of a supply chain member (Titman and Wessels 1998). In addition, limited incidence of trade credit exposure in the creditor's balance sheet can significantly increase insolvency risk due to the combined effect of credit loss and the fall in demand (Jacobson and Von Schevdin 2015). Nonetheless, suppliers of standardized goods can be reluctant to extend trade credit to downstream customers as well because of the high risk of diversion, depending on whether the resale value of the assets is high and the possibility of replacing the supplier. Therefore, impact along the supply chain depends on the position of the firm in the network. However, to counterbalance the negative effect of credit chains in propagating shocks, it has been noted that, during crises, repeated business interactions can compensate for a lack of trust in suppliers and exposure to their extreme uncertainty. Therefore, the increase of credit risk is mitigated through the buyer's relationship with the supplier (Menichini 2011).

The tendency of interfirm relationships to generate portfolio losses is significantly influenced by firms' dependence on common macroeconomic factors (Giesecke and Weber 2004). In this case, multisourcing strategies are ineffective in preventing supply chain disruptions, because industry suppliers can go out of the business at the same time (Wagner et al. 2008), even though, in the case of contagion, the impact can be asymmetric with respect to macro conditions (Cardoso-Lecourtois 2004). Outside a single industry, the magnitude of the propagation of shocks along the supply chain can be affected by credit linkages between industries. Empirical evidence shows that an increase in direct trade credit relationships among industries significantly increases output correlations and an increase of bank credit related to trade credit is able to reduce sector comovements. Moreover, the comovements between sectors deriving from trade credit usage can also manifest themselves through links mediated by other industries (Raddatz 2010).

Conclusions

Traditional theories are still relevant in explaining trade credit usage, even though a better comprehension of their role requires a more detailed focus on other characteristics. Trade credit offers for price discrimination are sensitive to cross-sectional contexts; the larger the supplier size, the greater the trade-off between trade credit and inventory holdings. On the other hand, the support of sales through the offer of trade credit is found to be crucial for small and medium-sized enterprise debtor investments, which in turn reward suppliers with loyalty in business transactions and a liquidity premium on the purchase price. During monetary shortages, substitution between bank credit and trade credit works for firms regardless of size, even though the magnitude of the contribution in smoothing the credit channel is greater for small and medium-sized firms and is affected by the technology. For suppliers, trade credit offers are found to be effective in obtaining better financing conditions and lowering collateralization requirements in loan extensions by other creditors.

The importance of the relevance of trade credit in facilitating business transactions has fostered the introduction of a new coordinating mechanism among firms: Under financial constraints, a combination of a markdown allowance and financial debt will not help achieve the optimal order size because of positive financial costs. This is particularly the case when the retailer's cost of capital is high. Therefore, trade credit plays a principal role among inventory financing sources, whereas bank loans can be considered residual. Nonetheless, the coordinating role of trade credit can be hampered by market power along the supply chain: Powerful firms can demand generous payment terms or impose tight payment terms even if they are not financially constrained. Financial services targeted at supply chains are intended to waive market power in interfirm relationships.

Market power can be particularly relevant to firms in emerging countries participating in international supply chains, where the extension of trade credit is crucial to overcome the lack of financial flows provided by financial institutions in the transition toward a market economy. Moreover, in some geographical contexts, trade credit contributes to building a firm's profitability.

The usage of trade credit can assume unexpected patterns during a crisis. The initial growth determined by the substitution with a declined offer of bank credit ended shortly after the spread of the crisis. The global financial crisis of 2007-2008 showed the impact of a combination of idiosyncratic shocks and bank credit shortage in propagating distress along credit chains, following both upstream and downstream patterns. Only suppliers unconstrained before the start of the crisis were able to stop chain defaults, even though they were not immune from the reverse effect represented by the loss of future earnings when the defaulted counterparties were not replaced in a timely fashion, particularly in the supply of differentiated goods. Suppliers' credit risk during crises is weakly mitigated by exploiting the trust built from repeated business interactions with customers. Credit contagion through supply chains spreads asymmetrically among members due to exposure to the relevant shock, but it can go beyond the borders of economic sectors and either directly or indirectly impact other sectors, depending on outstanding trade credit relationships compared with bank credit relationships.

CHAPTER 3

Trade Credit Financing Instruments

Introduction

In light of multiple motivations for the use of trade credit, firms tend to supply and receive trade credit at the same time, so the choice to engage in one of these activities could influence the other. Nonetheless, the mismatch between the terms of accounts receivable and payable can determine financial needs to be satisfied through external sources, as revealed by the vast complementary usage of trade debt and financial debt and the weak ability of firms to substitute bank credit with trade credit due to the different nature of the sources, particularly during crisis periods. External sources that can satisfy financial needs connected with the extension of trade credit pertain to both bank instruments (see Trade Credit Financing Instruments: A Taxonomy section) and market instruments (see Trade Credit and Self-Liquidating Exposure: The Relevance of the Debtor section). Bank intervention in intermediating trade credit can span the following solutions: self-liquidating instruments finalized to anticipate the value of existing and future trade credits (see Self-Liquidating Loans section), factoring services intended to offer a complete solution for the financial and management needs of both creditors and debtors as determined by the usage of trade credit (see Factoring section), the provision of guarantees in international trade (see International Trade Instruments section), and solutions that address the financial needs of supply chains (see Supply Chain Finance Instruments section). Recourse to markets to satisfy financial needs connected with trade credit extension allows these needs to be satisfied through both standardized and tailored approaches: Commercial papers are commonly issued by large individual suppliers (see Commercial Papers section); securitizations of purchased receivables allow multiple sellers to build up sufficiently large trade credit portfolios to tackle market demand (see Securitization of Receivables section); innovative solutions are offered through the meeting of finance and technology, generally referred to as crowdfunding, that allows for tailored funding solutions to be offered to both creditors and debtors, based on the market group to which they belong (see Crowdfunding section).

The review of financing instruments of trade credits shows that the legal and management contexts are not homogeneous: Different legal frameworks characterize the transfer of trade credits and recourse to the trade creditor (see Legal Features section), whereas operational management approaches differ among financial instruments (see Operational Features section). Concluding remarks are presented in Conclusions section.

Trade Credit Financing Instruments: A Taxonomy

Bank Instruments

Self-Liquidating Loans

Self-liquidating loans finance preexisting commercial relationships; thus, the financial relationship has a trilateral and self-settling nature, particularly when there is no economic/juridical connection between suppliers and customers.

Banks can anticipate the value of trade credits through invoice discounting: The supplier assigns invoices to a bank that anticipates the discounted value, where the difference with respect to the nominal value is a function of both interest and fees. To elaborate, interest increases with maturity and the risk of the receivables, whereas fees are awarded by the bank to the collection service and can compensate the bank for excessively short maturities of receivables. The bank holds the right to encash the remittances of trade debtors, and, most of the times, it also has recourse to the assignor in case the trade debtor is delinquent on the due date. If the seller and customer have agreed to issue enforceable titles for the extension of delayed payments and the trade debtor fails to pay past dues on the receivables, the bank can directly initiate the recovery procedure through the competent court. Suppliers can also decide to maintain ownership of the trade credit and delegate the bank for collection. The nominal value of the receivables can be made available before maturity by increasing the overdraft limit, and any past due amounts will immediately lower the supplier's available credit limit.

Receivables financing solutions are particularly important in the United Kingdom, where invoice discounting represents more than 80 percent of all advances of receivables, with an increasing trend over time (Figure 3.1).

Factoring

Factoring is a management service and a financial technique that addresses enterprises' needs as determined by trade credits. Trade credits are assigned by the seller to the factor within the context of the commercial policy of the firm, and a major component of a factor's activity is, indeed, the management of credits. In addition to the management of trade credits, upon the seller's request, the factor can provide the following services: financing, guarantee against the debtor's risk of default, and full services, that is, complete outsourcing to the factoring company of any needs determined by trade credit extension. For financing service, the factor anticipates between 60 and 80 percent of the nominal value of the assigned trade credit. In pro soluto factoring transactions, that is, without recourse to the assignor, the factor guarantees the success of the transaction, since it assumes the payment risk of the assigned debtor. If the assignor is not interested in obtaining an advance on the assigned trade credits, a maturity factoring transaction is realized. The assigning customer could deem it more effective and efficient to outsource completely any needs arising from the investment in trade credits to the factor, which has the required know-how. The firm thus has access to all the services already mentioned and maximizes the demand for managing activities, such as accounting, information, and collection services. Factoring services can be accessed without notification to the debtor. Therefore, non-notification factoring transactions can be agreed upon and the debtor will continue to pay trade debt to the assignor, who will encash trade credits in favor of the factor.

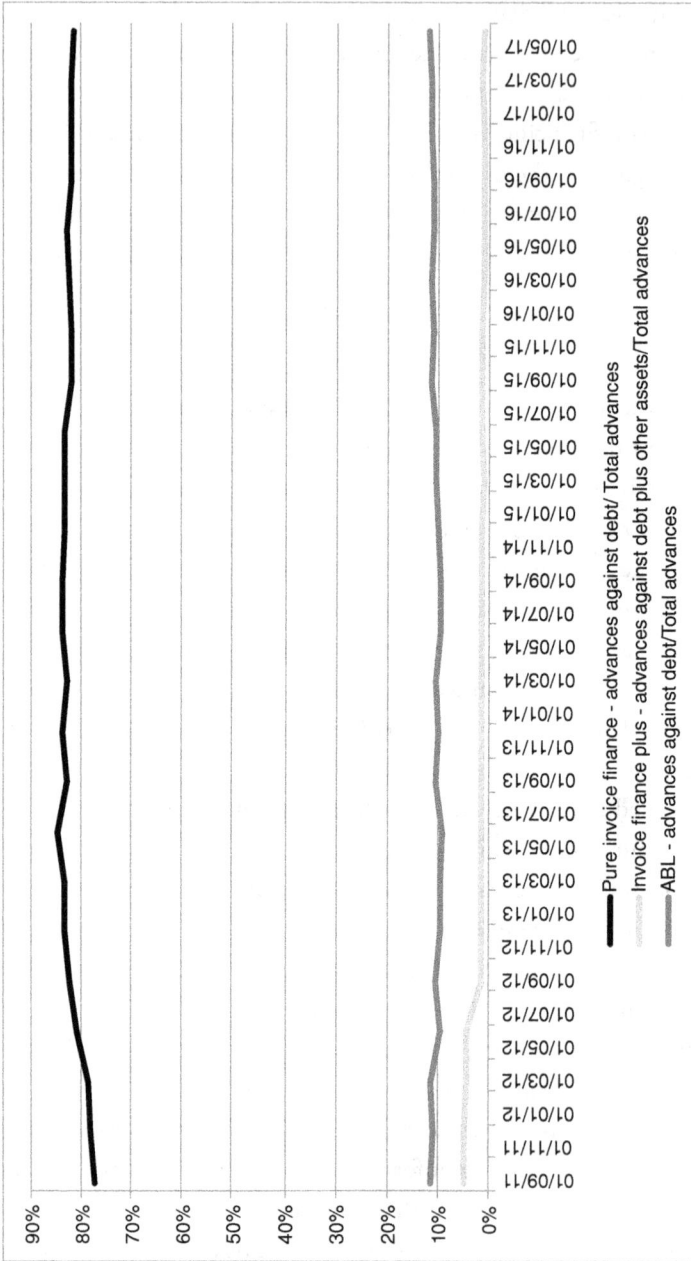

Figure 3.1 Receivables financing in the United Kingdom

Source: Author's elaborations of the U.K. finance data.

The chart legend reads:

- Pure invoice finance - advances against debt/ Total advances
- Invoice finance plus - advances against debt plus other assets/Total advances
- ABL - advances against debt/Total advances

Recently, an increasing number of large buyers have been accessing factoring services through the reverse factoring products (van der Vliet et al. 2015). To grant more lenient payment terms, buyers facilitate the early payment of trade credit obligations to suppliers by guaranteeing that the payment obligation will be met (Klapper 2006). This guarantee allows the factor to offer financing at a rate as low as the one that would be offered to the buyer. Investment-grade firms can therefore use reverse factoring to realize a significant reduction in the cost of credit for their suppliers.

Factoring volumes for European countries (Figure 3.2)—which, at the aggregate level, represent more than 60 percent of the world turnover[1] of domestic factoring (Factors Chain International 2017)— show that recourse and nonrecourse factoring at the European level carry the same weight, while strong variability can be observed at the country level. For example, in Germany, also because of legal matters, nonrecourse factoring represents the totality of the market. Reverse factoring appears to be very popular in the Iberian countries, whereas detailed data show that maturity factoring is a quite common practice in Italy. Last, the importance of international factoring transactions varies greatly among countries, whereas bank offers are almost equally distributed across all countries, comprising the entire market in some countries.

International Trade Instruments

Traditional trade finance products have been in existence in some form or the other for hundreds of years. Generally, banks act as intermediaries that facilitate the flow of documents (information) and payments related to the flow of goods in international trade or that provide assurance relating to the performance of financial obligations of one person or company

---

[1]The turnover is the value of all receivables assigned/sold to the factor by assignors during the reporting period, net of credit notes (EU Federation, 2017a).

31 December 2016	Total	International[d]	Non recourse[d]	Not notification[d]	Maturity Factoring[d]	Reverse Factoring[d]	Made by banks and banking groups[d]
Austria	19.621	42,0%	62,3%				100,0%
Belgium	62.846	49,2%	38,9%	56,3%			
Bulgaria	1.947	20,0%					
Croatia	2.825	4,8%					
Cyprus	2.925	0,9%					
Czech Republic	4.848	36,8%	37,7%				97,6%
Denmark	13.237	45,7%					
Estonia	2.495	17,2%					
Finland	22.000	9,1%					
France	268.160	29,3%	99,0%	53,3%			96,6%
Germany[a]	216.878	31,3%	39,8%	18,5%	4,7%	1,3%	100,0%
Greece	12.782	14,1%					
Hungary	3.635	8,7%					
Italy	208.642	23,5%	72,5%	36,9%	22,6%	5,0%	90,6%
Latvia	867	24,9%					
Lithuania	3.100	51,6%					
Luxemburg	339						
Malta	275	74,5%					100,0%
Netherlands	82.848	19,5%	48,5%	9,3%	0,1%	11,8%	89,3%
Poland	39.756	18,9%	27,3%			34,6%	
Portugal	24.517	14,1%					
Romania	4.016	19,5%					
Slovakia	1.646	0,5%					
Slovenia	1.000	12,7%					
Spain	130.656	16,5%	27,3%			48,0%	99,2%
Sweden	20.481	2,8%					
United Kingdom and Ireland[b]	350.830	8,1%	13,2%				
EU[c]	1.503.170	21,9%	48,3%	-	-	-	95,8%

Figure 3.2 Turnover volume by product allocation and notification

[a]No exact data for the German market are available, but nonrecourse factoring generally dominates due to Germany's legal factoring framework.

[b]Detailed figures for the United Kingdom and Ireland are only available in aggregated form.

[c]The EU figure is a weighted average, where the weight is the country turnover.

[d]Data are expressed as a percentage of the country total.

Source: EU Federation (2017b).

to another. Different products provide importers and exporters with various levels of risk mitigation and/or financing. These can be classified as follows (BAFT-IFSA 2011):

- Collection services
- Letters of credit
- Letters of guarantee
- International factoring

Collection services concern banks' handling of documents, in accordance with instructions, to obtain payment and/or acceptance, to deliver documents against payment and/or acceptance, or to deliver documents on other terms and conditions. Specifically, when collections of sales are payable on sight immediately, they are called documents against payment. These documents are sent to the presenting/drawee bank and delivered to the drawee against payment. Collection can allow the importer to pay at a future date through the delivery of documents against the debtor's acceptance. Depending on the agreements between the exporter and the importer, such a commitment can be supported by the issuance of a promissory note or draft drawn upon the purchaser by the seller. If this commitment to pay at a future date is accepted by the drawee/buyer, it is known as a trade acceptance.

A letter of credit is an irrevocable arrangement and thereby constitutes the issuing bank's undertaking to honor a presentation (Eun and Rensik 2018). Two types of letters of credit can be issued, documentary and commercial, as well as standby letters of credit. A documentary or commercial letter of credit is typically used to ensure payment for a transaction requiring the movement of goods and involves the presentation of commercial documents that usually transfer the title of the underlying goods. Standby letters of credit are typically used as performance or financial assurances and are payable against a simple demand or against a demand and a statement.

Under clearly prescribed conditions, a bank guarantee is a bank's irrevocable promise to compensate the beneficiary fully, immediately, and without fail for damages suffered in the event of default by the applicant of the letter of guarantee. Guarantees are usually governed by local law and different International Chamber of Commerce (ICC) rules.

The product mix between export and import finance (Figure 3.3) shows that the prevailing instrument is the commercial letter of credit, whereas standby letters of credit are, as expected, more relevant to exports than to imports. The usage of bank guarantees differs greatly between export and import finance. In the latter, greater recourse to guarantees compensates for the lower demand for standby letters of credit. Open account transactions show the same relevance in both export and import finance and are frequently backed by supply chain services (see Supply Chain Finance Instruments section).

In the international context, factoring deploys the typical services of the operation, and, therefore, the structure of the transaction is more complex. Differences in the domiciles of the exporter and importer require the intervention of two corresponding factors that can make the risk of the transaction affordable: Financial, guarantee, and collection services are indirectly provided to the exporter by the factor of the importer in the best position to evaluate risks, and, conversely, the importer can access international factoring services to delay the exporter's payments. To satisfy purely financial needs, factors offer export invoice discounting products.

International factoring accounts for roughly 20 percent of the world's factoring. This share has increased over time, consistent with the global recovery after the global financial crisis (Figure 3.4). In terms of product, export factoring dominates the international factoring market and the increase in export invoice discounting corresponds to the decrease in import factoring.

Supply Chain Finance Instruments

A distinct role for trade credit has emerged in coordinating supply chains (see Chapter 2). Therefore, solutions addressing emerging financial and managing needs are offered through supply chain finance services, defined as follows (Global Supply Chain Finance Forum 2016, p. 8):

> Supply chain finance is defined as the use of financing and risk mitigation practices and techniques to optimise the management of the working capital and liquidity invested in supply chain processes and transactions. Supply chain finance is typically applied

Export and Import trade finance mix by product

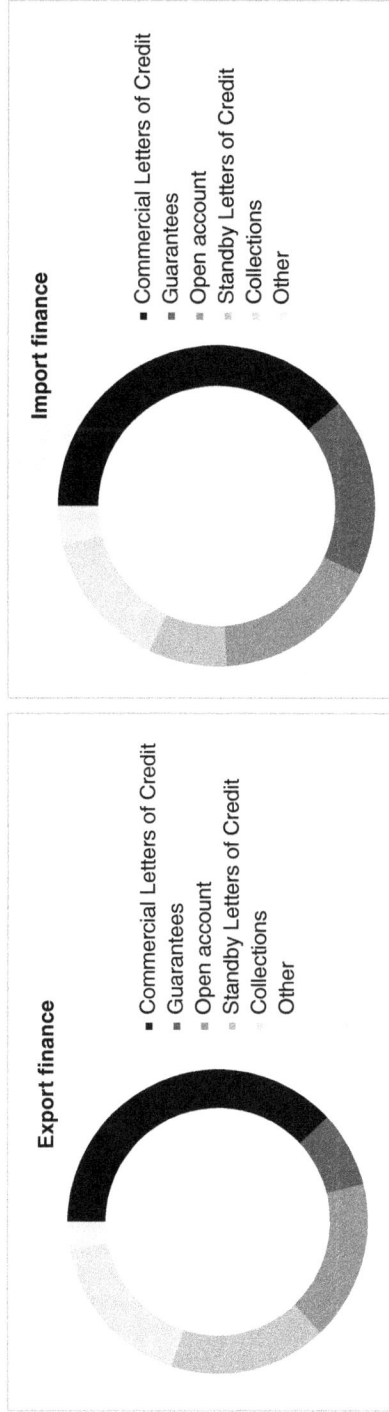

Figure 3.3 Export and import trade finance mix, by product

Source: Author's elaborations of ICC data (2016).

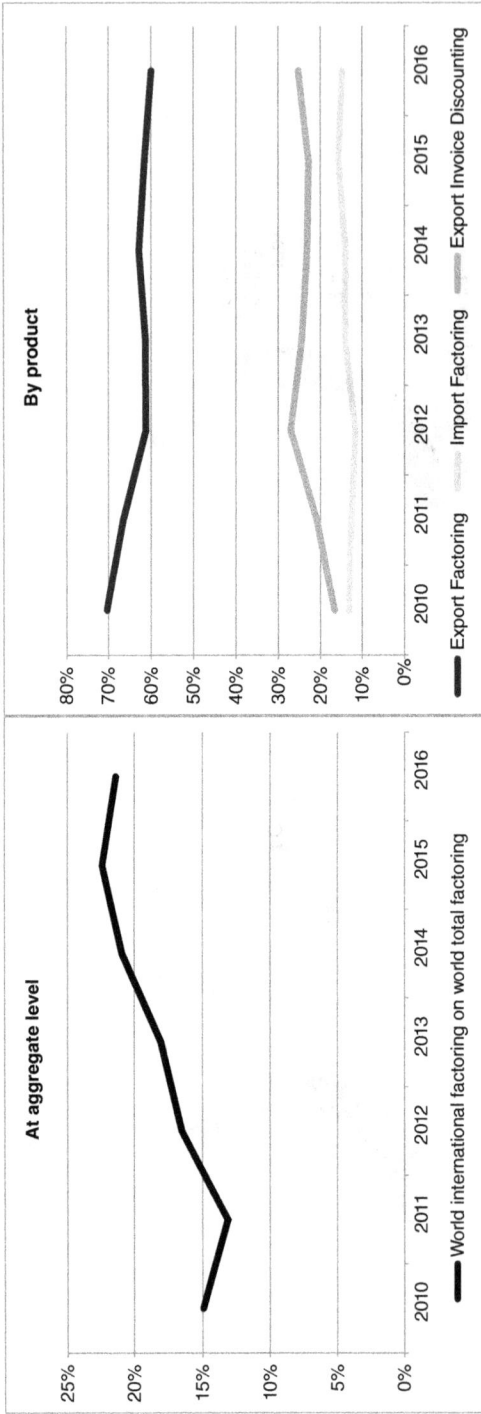

Figure 3.4 International factoring

Source: Author's elaborations of Factors Chain International data (2017).

to open account trade and is triggered by supply chain events. Visibility of underlying trade flows by the finance provider(s) is a necessary component of such financing arrangements which can be enabled by a technology platform.

Supply chain finance services allow companies to exchange goods and services without advancing cash and, in international trade, without resorting to documentary credit. Flows of goods and services between parties activate the provision of supply chain services through the posting of orders, invoices, and other sort of claims. To address the parties' changing needs, flexible supply chain finance services are offered based on a combination of traditional and innovative financing techniques. In particular, services concerning the financing of trade credits can be classified as follows:

- Receivables purchase. This category encompasses receivables discounting, forfeiting,[2] factoring, and payables finance.
- Loans or advances. This category groups both loans for future trades and advances against receivables. The distributor can also benefit from a bridge loan to match the resale to the retailer or the final customer. Last, the warehousing and holding of inventories and goods can be financed, as well as purchase orders, from a reputable buyer through pre-shipment finance.

Currently, the most common technique in supply chain finance is receivables discounting (Figure 3.5). Generally, firms use supply chain finance instruments of trade credit more than inventory and fixed capital financing.

Supply chain finance services are expected to be the most important area for fostering the growth of trade finance in the coming years (ICC 2017). More recently, interbank transactions have made supply chain

---

[2]Forfeiting is a type of medium-term trade financing used to finance the sale of capital goods. Forfeiting involves the sale of promissory notes signed by the importer in favor of the exporter. The forfeit buys the promissory notes from the exporter at a discount. The exporter can thus satisfy the financial needs associated with the sale.

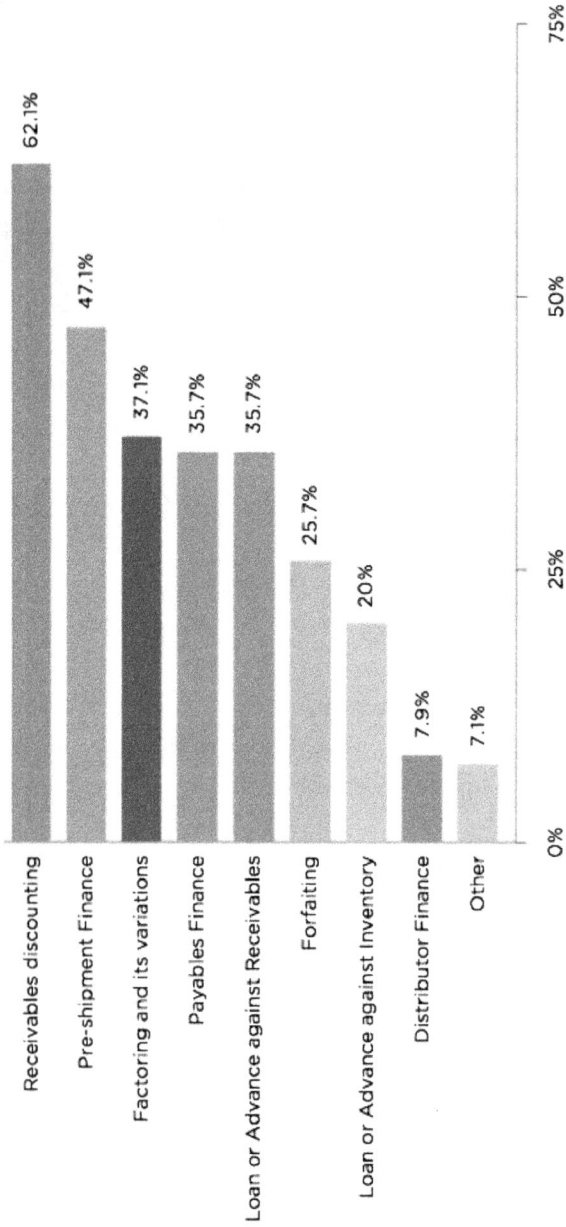

Figure 3.5 *Most common techniques in supply chain finance*

Notes: The percentages are the proportions of different techniques as determined from the ICC Global Survey on Trade Finance 2017.

Source: ICC (2017).

finance services available in open trade account agreements through a framework that enables bank payment obligations (Meijer and Menon 2012). A bank payment obligation is

> An irrevocable and independent undertaking of an obligor bank to pay or incur a deferred payment obligation and pay at maturity a specified amount to a recipient bank following submission of all data sets required by an established baseline and resulting in a data match or an acceptance of a data mismatch. (ICC 2013, p. 7)

The parties involved in the framework are represented by the buyer and the buyer's bank on one side, and the seller and the seller's bank on the other. Under a conditional payment mechanism based on matching the trade dates on an electronic platform, the instrument can be issued to make immediate payments or deferred payments, based on the irrevocable undertaking of the obligor bank toward the recipient bank. In the baseline, the commercial data elements to be agreed upon by the buyer and seller as the basis for triggering the payment obligation and any subsequent financing are defined, and any mismatch will prevent the bank obligation from becoming due, unless the buyer explicitly authorizes the payment (Swift 2015).

Market Instruments

Commercial Papers

Receivables are assets that, because of their properties, can also be the target of market investments. Traditionally, large U.S. suppliers finance their receivables through the issue of commercial papers, that is, short-term and unsecured instruments (Alsworth and Borio 1993). The instrument's maturity does not exceed 3 months, with a prevailing maturity not exceeding 60 days (Adrian et al. 2011) and the highest percentage of issues characterized by a maturity not exceeding 4 days (Table 3.1). Most of the offers are made by highly rated issuers because market demand is very sensitive to the issuer's credit risk, and low-quality issuers therefore will not risk under-raising funds (Calamoris et al. 1995): In addition to firm's operating results and financial structure, rating agencies also apply more subjective criteria, such as the quality of management and industry characteristics (Hahn 1998). By investing in a pure discount instrument, investors can realize returns that compare with short-term interest rates and are affected by the issuer's credit risk, the rollover risk, and industry risk. Issuer credit risk can be offset through credit guarantees and, to mitigate rollover risk and associated liquidity crisis, issuers can back commercial papers through guarantees or, more frequently, bank loan commitments (Calamoris 1989).

Table 3.1 Volume statistics[a] for commercial paper issuance for AA nonfinancial issuers

Year	Total	1–4 days	5–9 days	10–20 days	21–40 days	41–80 days	81+ days
2015	6,135	3,973	833	369	460	317	183
2016	7,323	4,282	1,355	379	492	488	327
2017[b]	8,491	4,958	1,596	562	726	339	310

[a]Billions of dollars.
[b]Data through October 13.
Source: Board of Governors of the Federal Reserve System (2017).

Given the volume of domestic issues, a cross-border market of euro-commercial papers has developed that, nonetheless, lags behind the U.S. market due to its fragmented nature, lack of issuance standards, and weak secondary trading (Robin 2011).

Securitization of Receivables

Because trade receivables can be considered steady assets and associated with a predictable financial stream, they are eligible to be transferred through securitization. Commercial papers can also be issued by a conduit/special-purpose entity that purchases receivables. Therefore, such assets are segregated and bankruptcy remote with respect to the seller's balance sheet and bought on a revolving basis to replace expiring collateral (Murphy 2008). The conduit can buy receivables from an individual seller or connected sellers, called a single-seller conduit, or from a large number of independent sellers, a multi-seller conduit. Regardless of the type of conduit, the management of the sponsoring bank decides on which asset portfolios to buy. Since individual assets can remain unknown, traditional commercial papers can be considered less transparent and more complex.

The seller(s) obtains a price that is determined by giving a haircut to the nominal value of the sold receivables. Such a haircut leads to overcollateralization and is therefore a form of internal credit enhancement. Compared with commercial papers, the higher volumes issued over time are affected by the opportunity for lower-quality issuers to use the program to satisfy funding needs and, depending on local regulations, exploit the off–balance sheet treatment of the obtained funding (Bate et al. 2003). Sharing the same potential for risk as commercial papers do, rollover risk has been proven to be very important during the global financial crisis when runs were diffused, even though it was affected by observable program characteristics such as program type, sponsor type, and macrofinancial variables (Covitz et al. 2013). Because securitized assets originate in commercial transactions between the seller and trade debtors, past dues at maturity can be determined by both default risk and dilution risk, that is, the possibility that disputes about the commercial transaction can dilute the outstanding amount of credit due at maturity (Pilfer 1996).

The U.S. data (Figure 3.6) show that the market has strongly slowed down since the global financial crisis and current conditions appear still lower compared with 2001.

Crowdfunding

Previously identified market solutions to satisfy trade receivables financing needs require the intervention of a financial intermediary who extends various types of financial services and prevents the demand for allocating investments to single receivables or pools of receivables. This restriction can be overcome through peer-to-peer lending, which is based on online microloans between individuals without the intermediation of a financial institution (Carignani and Gemmo 2007). Individuals request funding from other creditors, who are mostly not professional investors (Borello et al. 2014), even though peer-to-peer lending could theoretically attract institutional savings (Hernando 2016). Peer-to-peer lending was adopted to finance trade receivables before the global financial crisis, giving rise to the term *peer-to-business* because of the corporate nature of the offering entities. After 2008, the number of such lending platforms increased dramatically (Everett 2014), and strong online lending made

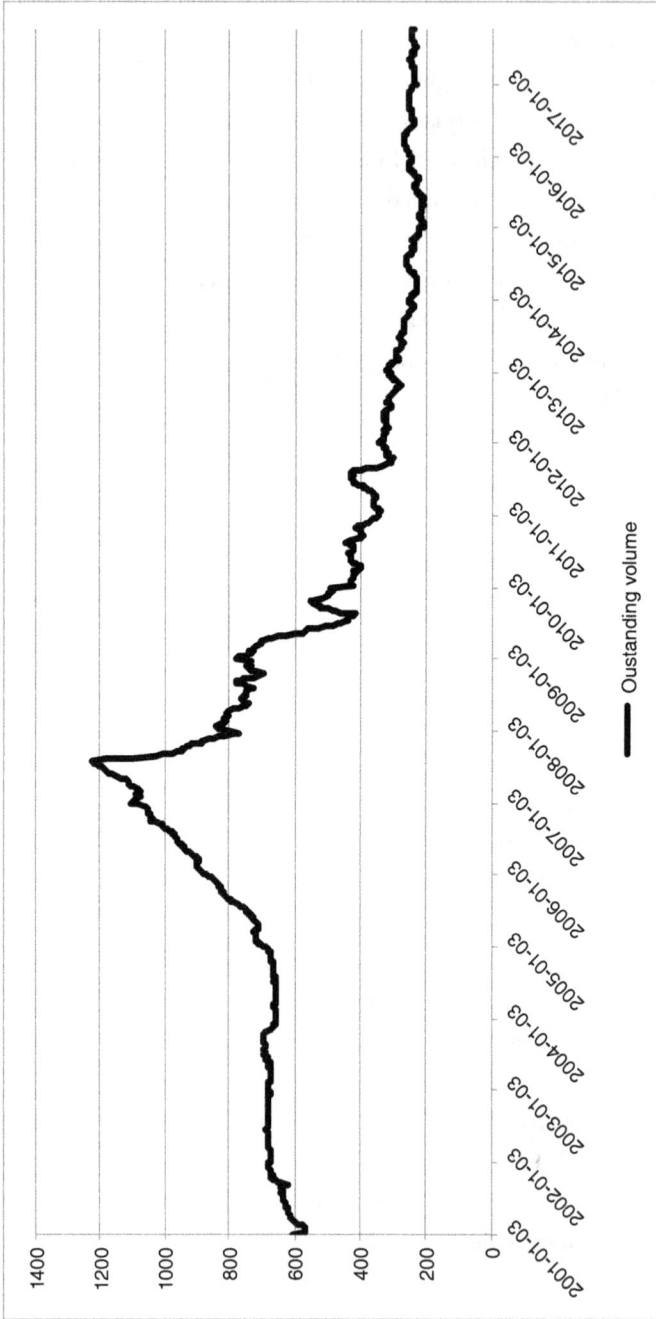

Figure 3.6 *Asset-backed commercial paper issues in the United States*

Note: The data are in billions of dollars and seasonally adjusted.

Source: Board of Governors of the Federal Reserve System (2017).

funds available to young and low-income businesses without government support (OECD 2015). In particular, different platforms of asset-based lending where borrowers could seek finance against receivables emerged in Anglo-Saxon countries, as in the case of the Receivables Exchange[3] in the United States and MarketInvoice in the United Kingdom. Currently, platforms specialized in receivables financing represent one of fastest-growing alternative finance models (Zhang et al. 2016). In the receivables financing marketplace, corporate debtors were initially mainly small firms, but the growing limitations of invoices that can be anticipated have made the solution attractive for medium firms as well. Currently, firms can anticipate funding in the range of 80 to 90 percent of the gross value of invoices. Depending on the firm's financial needs, it can choose a specific financial solution or finance the whole ledger. Generally, prerequirements on receivables involve the creditworthiness of trade debtors. Firms can also anticipate the value of future credits from contracts, licenses, and retainers. Firms pay an upfront fee as a percentage of the funds obtained (MarketInvoice 2017). Additional services can be offered by the platform to the firm, such as credit evaluation, insurance against customer default, and collections (Morse 2015). The innovation of the products offered by the platforms has extended the type of financial assets that can be traded by including more trade payables and letters of credit than receivables (LiquidX 2017).

The successful launch of crowdfunding initiatives in trade finance has witnessed extraordinary growth in crowdfunding since the inception of the volumes advanced by the most important player in Europe, Market-Invoice. Even after its introductory years, its average yearly growth rate still far exceeds 20 percent (Figure 3.7).

Trade Credit and Self-Liquidating Exposure: The Relevance of the Debtor

Legal Characteristics

The review of receivables financing solutions (see Trade Credit Financing Instruments: A Taxonomy section) has shown that various financiers will

---

[3]In 2016, LiquidX acquired the Receivables Exchange.

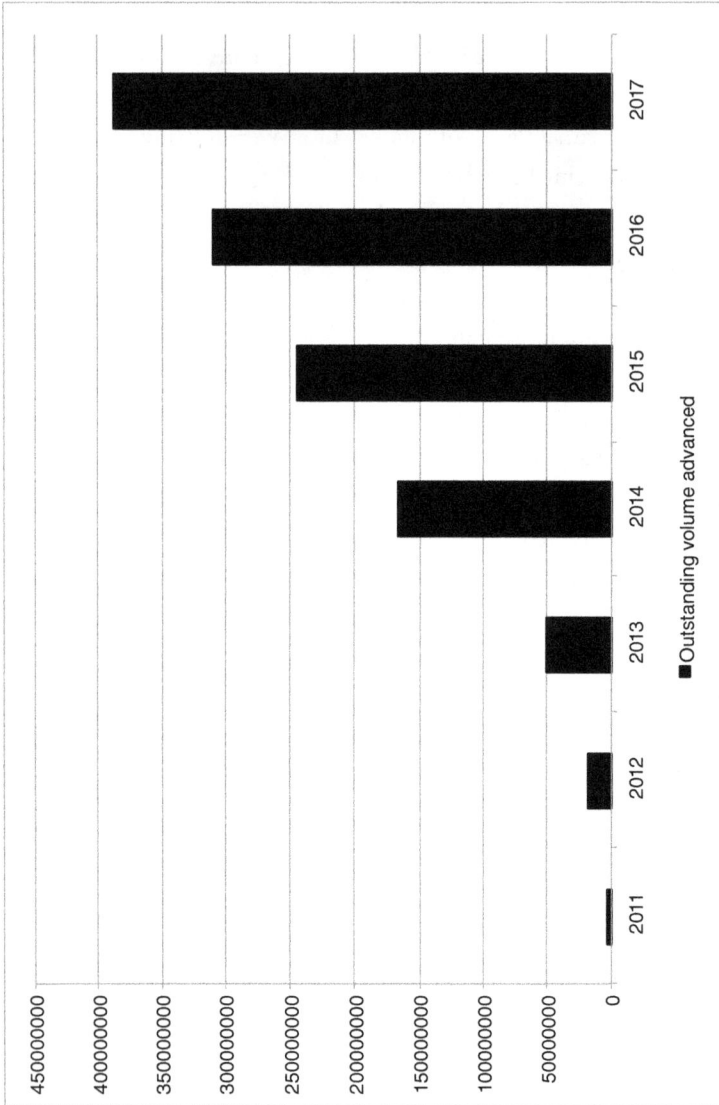

Figure 3.7 Evolution of volumes advanced by MarketInvoice

Note: The data are in british pounds.

Source: MarketInvoice (2017).

collect the reimbursement of the credit by the trade debtor because of the self-liquidating nature of the exposure. Nonetheless, different receivables financing solutions are characterized by different rights to recover the exposure of the trade debtor in the case of past dues and/or to ask the seller to pay for past due exposure. Such opportunities to mitigate financier's risk are determined by the legal framework of the financing operation. In particular, the following elements can be considered crucial in the definition of the counterparties by which the financier can recover unpaid exposure:

- The legal basis of the transfer of the receivables
- The right of recourse to the trade creditor

The aforementioned elements differ among bank and market instruments (Table 3.2). In the case of bank instruments, trade credit can be pledged in favor of the creditor, as in the case of self-liquidating loans, but excluding collection services authorized by the bank to hold encashed amounts; assigned to an assignee, as in the case of factoring; or sold in a true sale as an optional solution in supply chain finance services. In terms of market instruments, the transfer of trade credits through a true sale is most common. Both bank and market instruments have recourse to

Table 3.2 Legal framework across trade credit lending/financing instruments

Financial instrument of receivables	Legal transfer of trade credits	Right of recourse to the trade creditor
Self-liquidating loans	No/Yes	Yes
Factoring	Yes	Yes/No
International trade instruments	No	No
Supply chain finance instruments	Yes	No
Commercial papers	No	Yes
Securitization of receivables	Yes	No
Crowdfunding	Yes	Yes

Source: Author's elaborations.

trade creditor, mainly when the financier provides funds, and the offer of other managing services at the same time improves the trade debtor's knowledge and makes the risk affordable without the intervention of a trade creditor.

Operational Characteristics

While financial instruments differ according to their legal framework, they differ more because of the multiple operational approaches financiers use to manage trade debt. Generally, it is possible to identify the following three main approaches:

- Trade credits are regarded as collateral to back the trade creditor's financial exposure.
- Trade credits are regarded as the counterparty's exposure, regardless of recourse to the trade creditor in case of delinquency.
- Future trade credits are regarded as the expected turnover of trade creditor business.

According to the first approach, the financier manages trade credits at the portfolio level, limiting an ad hoc treatment to only more concentrated trade credits. Even though the financier acts as a collection service, any relationship with the trade debtor is maintained, because it is the relationship with the trade creditor that is being managed, of which the debtor is unaware. In other words, when trade debtors are the counterparty's exposure, the financier holds a direct relationship with them, managing the relationship from evaluation to collection. The financier can oppose all rights and exceptions to the trade debtor that the trade creditor would oppose. Lastly, an offer of the anticipated value of future credits from contracts, licenses, and retainers is managed as a loan to the trade creditor because the right to manage trade debtors must still be originated. Nonetheless, future credits contribute to the trade creditor's expected development, and, therefore, future trade credit relationships will be managed within the trade credit business.

Conclusions

Trade credit is a relevant asset for the development of trade finance. Firms can satisfy their financing needs through both bank and market instruments. In each category, firms can find instruments that combine different properties and value-added services, characterized by product and process innovations to satisfy emerging needs.

While moving away from traditional self-liquidating loans but still playing a crucial role in enabling firms to discount invoices, banks and financial intermediaries enrich pure financing services by allowing firms to outsource completely all needs connected with the management of trade receivables, as in the case of factoring. Factoring can be fruitfully used in international trade as a potential alternative to letter of credit and guarantees. Among financial services addressing international transactions, letter of credit plays an important role, even though open account transactions are increasing over time. The evidence can be interpreted in light of the increasing importance of supply chain finance services, a key driver in the development of future international trade, based on a combination of existing and new products by means of technological applications. The strategic relevance of supply chain finance has stimulated the offer of supply chain solutions through bank payment obligations, a service fully processed by means of interbank relationships.

Among market instruments, commercial papers still represent a core solution that satisfies the financial needs stemming from revolving receivables, even though sourcing funds are mainly available to high-quality issuers. The limitation of issuer quality is somewhat overcome through asset-backed commercial papers: The volumes of asset-backed commercial papers are much higher compared with other types of commercial papers, even though a strong downturn has been observed since the global financial crisis. In the past few years, an innovative alternative has emerged in the context of crowdfunding. The volumes anticipated through platforms focused on discounting invoices are growing very quickly, making invoice discounting one of the most important deals in peer-to-peer lending.

The products to finance trade credits reviewed in the preceding show that solutions differ according to the legal framework and operational approach. In particular, the legal framework affects the base of the transfer of receivables and recourse to the seller if the trade debtor is delinquent. Bank and market instruments are not clearly differentiated along legal characteristics. Operational characteristics affect the way trade credits are managed. Trade credits can therefore be either collateral or a counterparty of the exposure.

CHAPTER 4

Credit Risk Framework for Trade Credit Financing Exposure

Introduction

Trade finance represents an important lending portfolio for financiers. An important characteristic that attracts investments is the risk mitigation that trade receivables determine for lender exposure. Because trade finance is developed based on commercial relationships that existed prior to the origination of the lending exposure, evaluation of the risk mitigation determined by the trade credits requires an ad hoc approach in the development of a credit risk framework. In particular, the preexisting trade relationship, the legal framework governing the transfer of trade credits, and the management of receivables can affect the extent of risk mitigation for the lender (see Credit Risk Framework for Trade Credit Financial Instruments section).

The development of a credit risk framework is based on the potential sources of credit loss. Trade credit financing can expose financiers to losses determined by default events, as in other credit exposures, as well as by a distinct risk source characterizing such financing activity, that is, dilution risk (see Credit Risk Evaluation at Individual Level section).

At the aggregate portfolio level, concentration risk is crucial to the financier's stability. By financing trade credit and also trade debt, financiers can originate concentrated exposures arising from preexisting supply relationships. Therefore, proper interpretation of the application of standard approaches and the need for adaptation are required (see Credit Risk Evaluation at Portfolio Level: Concentration Risk section). Concluding remarks are presented in Conclusions section.

Credit Risk Framework for Trade Credit Financial Instruments

Credit risk is the risk of losses due to the debtor's inability to repay the borrowed capital and/or to pay the accrued interest (Bessis 2015). The obligor is unable to repay the debt and/or the accrued interest due to being in a default status, even though the obligor has not declared bankruptcy. A defaulted debtor is unable to pay any financial liabilities, and, therefore, default is an absorbing state (Dietch and Petey 2004). When the debtor does not repay the debt according to the agreed terms, even if the debtor can afford it, the debtor is commonly considered to be defaulting strategically (Guiso et al. 2013). In the case of exposure arising from trade credit financing, where the repayment of the debt is primarily based on trade debtor performance, different behaviors can be observed at each accrued term, even though the debtor is not defaulting strategically. Unlike financial exposure, the payment obligation of the trade debtor is subject to both terms and conditions related to the execution of the commercial transaction (Gibilaro 2004). Therefore, potential credit losses in trade credit financing instruments can arise from the following sources:

- Risk of default, that is, the state of insolvency of the counterparty obliged to repay the exposure. It is to be noticed that in trade credit financing instruments, because of the trilateral relationship between the trade creditor, the trade debtor, and the financier, the counterparty receiving the advance is not the counterparty primarily involved in the repayment of the debt. Only if the assignment of receivables is with recourse, the counterparty is responsible for it. In nonrecourse transactions, the default event concerns the insolvency of the trade debtor, even though the financial exposure of the financier is toward the seller/assignor that is not responsible for trade debtors' failure caused by the risk of dilution.
- Risk of dilution. This refers to the

  > Possibility that the receivable amount is reduced through cash or non-cash credits to the receivable's obligor. Examples include offsets or allowances arising from returns of goods sold, disputes regarding product quality, possible

> debts of the borrower to a receivables obligor, and any pay-
> ment or promotional discounts offered by the borrower
> (e.g., a credit for cash payments within 30 days). (Basel
> Committee on Banking Supervision 2004, p. 89)

> Dilution risk can determine credit losses as an alternative to default
> risk, since the financier cannot lose twice on the same exposure and
> the approaches to managing receivables can affect risk discovery.

Exposure to multiple credit risk sources makes credit evaluation more specific with respect to other short-term credit exposures. The specific characteristics of trade credit financing affect the planning of the entire credit risk management system.[1] Even though credit risk input parameters for internal rating systems and credit risk models apply to trade credit financing exposure, their estimation requires a preventive discussion of the specific issues from both the individual and portfolio credit risk perspectives.

Credit Risk Evaluation at the Individual Level

For each exposure arising from financing trade credit, the financier must obtain an assessment of credit risk that encompasses the assessment of both default risk and dilution risk. In such an evaluation, the following play crucial roles:

- The events associated with the risk manifestation
- The set of information and the approaches adopted to analyze the counterparty's creditworthiness

Default Risk

To assess default risk, a definition of default must be introduced. The definition of the default status must allow for the identification of the status of an obligor that attests to the fact that the obligor is unable to repay liabilities with the available assets and is constrained by the increase in

---

[1]For further details on credit risk management systems, see Resti and Sironi (2007).

existing liabilities (Beaver 1966). From both the management and regulatory perspectives, the number of events that infer a default status and lead to different exit strategies has grown (Bottazzi et al. 2011). Therefore, a counterparty can be classified as having defaulted because of material past dues, even if the counterparty has not been declared bankrupt by a competent court (Basel Committee on Banking Supervision 2004). Regarding credit exposure derived from financing trade credit where the payments are connected to commercial transactions characterized by terms and conditions, it is important to distinguish between the following:

- Delinquency. The trade debtor can be delinquent on payments connected with single invoices because of longer commercial terms in collecting payments from the buyers. Therefore, a regular delay for homogeneous commercial transactions at the sectorial level can be observed at each accrued maturity. The trade debtor can also be delinquent for motivations derived from dilution risk (see Dilution Risk section). Therefore, the missed payment does not originate from a decline in creditworthiness, and, if the dispute is resolved, it can manifest in the very short term.
- Default. Because default is an absorbing state, the obligor is expected to be past due with respect to the vast majority of accrued terms, including those deriving from receivables that originated from commercial transactions with different suppliers.

The evaluation of default risk concerns both the trade debtor and, in recourse operations and future credit financing, the seller/assignor, that is, the obligor, for the advanced amounts.

As in other lending facilities, the appraisal of default risk aims to forecast the creditworthiness of the counterparty through economic, financial, and assets and liabilities statements and both quantitative and qualitative information (De Laurentis 2001). The exact type of information to be selected will depend on the segment of the counterparty, which, on the trade debtor side, can be a firm,[2] a consumer,[3] or a local

---

[2]For a broader discussion on firm distress, see Altman and Narayanan (1997).
[3]For a broader discussion on consumer distress, see Crook et al. (2007).

public entity.[4] The information set is slightly enlarged through the acquisition of information concerning the procurement area. This information
is particularly valuable for financial groups because it is not shared with
other financiers controlled by the same financial holding company. In
greater detail, the type of information that trade credit financiers are able
to retrieve through at least monthly, if not more frequent, monitoring
activities includes the following:

- Invoices, with complete details (supplier name, and description
  of the supply, terms, and any exceptions ruling the commercial
  relationship)
- Payment dates
- Payment delays
- Any disputes about the supply (events to be reconciled with
  dilution risk)
- Any payments encashed directly by the seller/assignor and any
  delay in the forwarding of cash flows to the financier
- The flow of new sales/assignments of trade receivables

Procurement information is useful for the evaluation of default risk
from both the trade debtor's and the creditor's perspectives, even though
the interpretations differ. Analysis of the procurement information allows the integration of trade debtor information sources to examine the
following:

- The sourcing policy with respect to individual suppliers. The
  aggregation of information on individual supply relationships
  allows one to infer the relevance of the supplier to the trade debtor,
  and, therefore, the market power the trade debtor can impose on
  suppliers and the detection of value chain relationships (Klapper
  et al. 2012).
- The trade debtor's general payment behavior. In particular, it is
  possible to distinguish between the following:

---

[4]For a broader discussion on the distress of local public entities, see Jones and
Walker (2007).

- ○ Recurrent regular payment delays that originate from a longer encashment period in the output market with respect to the sourcing market. Moreover, such payment behavior can characterize debtors' allocated funds from collection whose duration is beyond their decisional power. Empirical evidence shows that this behavior characterizes central and local public administrations, particularly those in European Mediterranean countries (Connell 2014).
- ○ Inability of the trade debtor to pay multiple invoices or the undertaking of strategic behaviors. The information in invoices allows one to qualify any delinquent behavior due to the in-kind financing nature of trade credit (Bukart and Ellingsen 2004).

The usefulness of the information that can be retrieved from the procurement area also extends to the evaluation of the default risk of the seller/assignor. The financier can examine the following:

- The composition, concentration, and stability of the customer base, information that is particularly relevant to the projection of a firm's future growth
- The rate of growth through the monitoring of the flow of sales/ assignments of receivables
- The ability of trade creditors to impose strict terms on buyers by applying market power to downstream counterparties
- The satisfaction of the customer base with the trade creditor supply through the observation of disputes and the interpretation of such observations

Dilution Risk

The evaluation of dilution risk is a distinctive feature of trade credit financing. It affects the amount of potential losses, and it can have different causes (Modansky and Massimino 2011). Dilution risk can be assumed to be (Association Française des Sociétes Financières 2003) any of the following:

- An independent risk originating from deep within the procurement area and associated with disputes on the execution of the supply breaching agreed-upon quality and quantity standards. The risk manifests separately from other risk sources and is discovered during the supply or shortly after the trade debtor's payment deadline (Gibilaro 2006).
- A risk correlated with other risk sources. Given such a perspective, dilution risk can be both the following:
  - The short-term occurrence of default risk. The deterioration of the supplier's creditworthiness leads to lower-than-agreed-upon quality standards, creating customer disputes. At the same time, a financially constrained trade debtor can raise weak arguments to postpone payments to future dates.
  - A manifestation of operational risk.[5] The reduction of the receivables amount on the due date can be determined to be due to outside fraudulent actions taken by both the seller/assignor and the trade debtor.

Because of the strong differences between the causes of the risk, only the independent risk type is considered ordinary dilution, and the other types are referred to as exceptional dilution (Fédération Bancaire Française 2003).

The multiple reasons for dilution require segmentation and the information to evaluate the risk of potential losses. Dilution events result in either of the following:

- The receivable obligor's noncash credits to the seller/assignor determine the reduction of the outstanding amount of collectable trade credits.
- The receivable obligor's cash credits to the seller/assignor due to underperformance in the execution of the supply give rise to payments because of damages.
- Cash credits of the seller/assignor toward the receivable's obligor due to past due exposures are not supported by the discovery of other dilution causes.

---

[5]For a broader discussion on operational risk, see Chernobai et al. (2007).

A representative list of dilution causes segmented by dilution type is presented in Table 4.1.

Table 4.1 Dilution type and dilution events

Dilution type	Dilution events
Ordinary dilution	• Allowances from the return of the goods sold • Disputes regarding product quality and quantity • Payments for promotional discounts offered by the borrower • Offsets from unintentional damages
Default risk–related dilution	• Nonpayment of installments • Subcontractor's direct collection
Operational risk–related dilution	• Offsets from reciprocal receivables • Anticipated invoices • Multiple assignments • Forgery of documents • Invoices on counterfeit or fraudulent goods • For undisclosed agreements, commingling

Source: Author's elaborations.

Even though the events summarized in Table 4.1 are representative and do not represent numerous possible causes, they depict completely different situations. Therefore, evaluation of the risk of dilution requires ad hoc approaches.

Ordinary dilution is strictly connected with the normal relationship between the seller/assignor and the trade debtor during the procurement execution. The dilution event manifests mainly as the receivable's obligor's noncash credit. The financier can isolate dilution causes because the events are expected to be resolved in the short run, typically under 90 days, in favor of the trade debtor or the seller/assignor (Assifact 2012).

Evaluation of the risk of ordinary dilution requires the appraisal of multiple supply characteristics. In particular, evaluation of the risk of returned goods considers the following (Gibilaro 2006):

- The type of good and the connected market segment
- The length of the commercial relationship between the transferor and the commercial debtor and the presence of performance clauses in the supply contract

Capital goods are high-value products, and their ability to satisfy buyer needs is affected by technological innovation and maintenance services (Pilcer 1996). Dilution events related to the return of goods sold can be caused by the obsolescence of the capital good and/or the failure to deliver the expected quality in the service relationship. Moreover, if the customer is sourcing parts or additional services from the seller of the capital good, the return can also affect the receivables connected with the procurement of additional supplies.

Regarding consumer goods, evaluation of the risk of return is particularly relevant in transactions with retailers (Bate et al. 2003). Given equal regulations, the risk increases exponentially when the item sold is affected by fashion and trends in consumer behavior that can lead to buyer's remorse shortly after purchase. The return of goods can manifest far beyond buyer's remorse: Retailers can return goods because of improper inventory management by the manufacturer or a distributor who fails to deliver goods at the proper time. Such dilution causes can be particularly relevant when the good in question is perishable and is generally characterized by a short shelf life, such as newspapers, pharmaceutical products, and seasonal products. Return practices can also give the retailer unlimited rights to return goods because of the nature of the goods. Retailers can also dilute the receivables assigned by the seller/assignor because of fees applied for multiple reasons, such as the following:

- Cooperative advertising of a new product
- Slotting allowances, particularly for food vendors
- Exclusive vendor arrangements to ensure privileged placement in a department store

A long-term relationship between a supplier and trade debtor can determine dilution events when the delivery of predefined goods is agreed upon but fails to take place (DeSimone and Moscowitz 2004). In particular, such long-term contracts can contain performance clauses concerning the quantity and price of the supply. Therefore, unattended behavior by the seller can result in dilution events.

Dilution events determined by the extension of price discounts can originate from the commercial policy of the seller/assignor. Promotional activities that can determine a price reduction are affected by the policy toward retailers, such as the following:

- Volume rebates offered by the manufacturer/distributor to the retailer based on customer purchases
- Loss-sharing agreements with the retailer
- Prompt payment discounts

Another case involves unanticipated requests of offsetting by the trade debtor because of damages caused by the sourced capital good. Regardless of the legal enforceability of offsetting, it is more convenient for the supplier to honor such requests in order to collect the residual receivables, by determining a reduction in the amounts to be collected.

The ordinary dilution events described above have different levels of likelihood and can therefore be classified as follows (Katz and Blatt 2008):

- Variable dilution, that is, events originating from disputes and post-sale negotiations with the obligors. This category of events is of great concern for financiers, because they tend to arise in worst-case termination scenarios. Therefore, this category contributes to the variability of dilution risk over time. The impact of such risk components can be mitigated through notification of the assignment and by limiting the provision of the advance to what the trade debtor will accept.
- Contractual dilution is essentially any reduction in the expected payment of a receivable that is known or contractually limited at the time the invoice is created. To this category belong volume rebates, discounts for prompt payments, and, generally, any expected noncash credit in the contract ruling the commercial relationship. Historical observations of the impact of such dilution events on outstanding receivables determine the expected dilution rate.
- Nondilutive credit is the substitution of an issued invoice with a new invoice due to errors, transfers, or reversals. The situation is said to be nondilutive because there is no new sale, only a substituting invoice. Since these events are determined by the extension of price discounts, they can originate from the commercial policy of the seller/assignor.

Moving on from going concern to exceptional dilution types, dilution can be the short-term manifestation of the default of both the seller and the trade debtor. The critical issue is the separation of dilution events of this type with respect to other types. The trade credit financier can distinguish them through monitoring activities that allow the financier to track payment performance with respect to multiple deadlines:

a) Diffused past dues with respect to the receivables for different trade debtors. This situation is expected to mirror a deterioration in the creditworthiness of the seller/assignor that reflects poor performance in the supply.

b) Diffused past dues of trade debtors with respect to receivables sold/ assigned by different sellers/assignors. The trade debtor is disputing the standards of the supplies because of the inability to pay and not because of ordinary dilution. In addition to disputes, such types of dilution can arise when the trade debtor attempts to encash directly from the customers in subcontracting relationships.

The evaluation of default-related dilution risk is based on information instrumental to evaluate default risk (see Default Risk section). The credit rating obtained by either the financier or an external vendor can be used to evaluate such dilution.

The causes of the last type of exceptional dilution pertain to operational risk. The isolation of such dilution causes requires analysis of the complete set of monitoring information. Events that could be labeled as ordinary dilution or default-related dilution could hide fraudulent actions perpetuated by either the seller/assignor or the trade debtor or both to the detriment of the financier. In particular, whereas an individual fraudulent action could be discovered upon the complaint of the trade debtor about the payment request, joint fraudulent action between the commercial counterparties can remain hidden for a long time. The financier's monitoring activities offer a broad, updated picture of the status of receivables payments. Therefore, the following behaviors at the supplier–buyer relationship level could be considered a proxy for risk:

- The number/amount of sales/assignments and the concurrent emergence of noncash credits to the debtor due to disputes about the standards of the supply
- The relationship between the turnover of sold/assigned receivables and the total sales of the supplier and buyer
- The sudden interruption of sales/assignments and failure to collect outstanding credits

In undisclosed sales/assignments of receivables, the seller/assignor is delegated by the financier to collect credits and forward the collected sum within a time limit: If the seller/assignor defaults before forwarding the collected sum to the seller, the risk of commingling arises. In this case, the dilution event is determined by mixture between the sum and the funds of the seller, with damages for the financier (BNP Paribas 2003).

The evaluation of the type of dilution discussed is based on causal operational risk factors, that is, inadequacies and failures in internal processes, people, and systems or external events (Basel Committee on Banking Supervision 2006). Among the different operational risk event types, external fraud and internal systems play a major role. The prevention of such events is the function of the implementation of adequate procedures and the adoption of effective legal remedies in the selling/assignment of trade credits. Concerning undisclosed agreements, the financier can limit the impact of the risk by avoiding or suspending delegation of the collection of receivables when the seller's risk of default is considered high.

Credit Risk Evaluation at the Portfolio Level: Concentration Risk

The risk that each sold/assigned receivable determines for the financier builds up specific credit portfolio risk at the aggregate level. Increasing the number of customers and applying classical principles to diversify a portfolio of financial activities is expected to decrease the relevance of the specific risk (Santomero 1997) in a way that is more than merely proportional to the decrease in performance that could be connected with such a diversification strategy (Deng and Elyasiani 2008).

Exposure to specific credit portfolio risk is assessed by taking into account the portfolio's level of concentration and adopting either a single-name measurement approach or one based on sectorial/geographical characteristics (Kamp et al. 2005). The first approach assumes that the characteristics of the financier's debtors are so heterogeneous that the concentration risk can only be assessed by considering the exposure from each debtor. High concentration levels raise issues concerning the possibility of collusion (Boot 2000) and the risk of illiquidity of the assets (Cerasi and Daltung 2000), even though these maximize creditor recovery when dealing with distressed firms (Bris and Welch 2005).

The hypothesis of establishing a univocal relationship between the business cycle and the performance of enterprises significantly limits debtor assessment models (Gordy 2003). It is possible to identify the relationships between the economic sector and/or the geographic area of the firm and sensitivity to the evolution of the reference scenario (Hanson et al. 2005). The approach based on sectorial/geographical profiles singles out within a credit portfolio those individuals who are homogeneous in respect of a few characteristics deemed relevant and show the same level of exposure upon the occurrence of a few significant external events (Altman and Saunders 1998). A high level of creditworthy debtor homogeneity implies the financier's excessive exposure to the risk of significant losses due to the propagation of generalized crises affecting enterprises in special sectors and/or geographical areas (Giesecke and Weber 2006). The presence of a level of structural concentration in a few sectors of economic activity could affect the financier who, over time, has gained distinct expertise working with select counterparty typologies (Stomper 2006). The credit portfolio can therefore characterize a level of structural geographic concentration (Carling and Lundberg 2002). Last, the financier characteristics affect the relevance of the two concentration measurement approaches, because the larger the entity, the lower the importance of name concentration in credit losses (Heitfield et al. 2005). Moreover, the customer base of the financier is maintained. For retail intermediaries, sectorial/economic concentration is more relevant, whereas single-name concentration is considered more important for corporate-oriented intermediaries (Kozak 2015) and, in the case of small and medium-sized enterprises, does not pose a risk below a critical granularity level (De Laurentis et al. 2017).

Concentration risk measurement approaches seem to focus on the creditor's exposure resulting from the debtor's financial liabilities, whereas the discovery of the relationship between the type of financial instrument and the approach to predict future losses is more recent. Within the context of the single-name approach, the financier's concentration toward a counterparty could result in significant losses with an exposure of a financial nature. In that case, the cause of the relationship is the debtor's financial needs, and repayment depends exclusively on the debtor's ability to generate cash flow. When the assessment of concentration risk concerns financial transactions based on trade credits, prior investigation into the basic reason for granting commercial credit is required. The literature cites two types of reasons that underlie the use of trade credit: financial determinants and real determinants (see Chapter 2). Should the financial reasons prevail, analogies with respect to the operations having a financial nature will predominate. On the contrary, should the real determinants prevail, use of the single-name approach will present analogies and divergences with respect to exposures having a definite financial nature.

From the former point of view, the financier who carries on transactions based on commercial credits could report large exposures to the supplier who transfers the credit or to the debtor who purchases the product/service. Unlike the financial exposures based on a bilateral relationship between lender and debtor, in trade credit financing, the relationship is based on a preexisting commercial relationship, and, therefore, the financial relationship is trilateral and self-settling.[6] Unlike the assessment of concentration for financial liabilities, the counterparty concentration of assets in such transactions does not entail exposure to the risk of greater losses with respect to a portfolio diversified on the side of the supplier–assignor and/or debtor–purchaser relationships. Even though the financier has great exposure to the seller/assignor, the repayment of the loan depends primarily on fulfillment on the part of trade debtors. If the large exposure is to the trade debtor, it is generally determined by the existence of supply relationships with more than one supplier, as well as by motivations determined by the optimization of the enterprise's financial

---

[6]The third-party relationship assumes the hypothesis of no economic/juridical connection between transferor and debtors.

structure. Analogous to what happens with respect to concentration risk involving the seller/assignor, a number of independent repayment sources exist. If the payment extensions from which a debtor benefits are, on average, longer than those admitted in its markets to replace the purchased goods and/or services (Dallocchio and Salvi 2004), they should allow the repayment of debts with benefits for the financier in terms of risk mitigation. Besides, it turns out that the moderate effectiveness of concentration risk control through the single-name approach is determined by the short original maturity of the trade credits, which is structurally less than 90 days. Based on the specificities of trade credit financing, single-name concentration risk control could be an effective tool to limit losses if measured within the portfolio of commercial credits that could be referred to each supplier. Debtor significance could imply an economic link between the seller/assignor and the supplier.

Regarding sectorial/geographic concentration risk in financial exposures, the effectiveness of such a tool is related to the influence exerted by the segmentation variables with respect to any trends in the creditworthiness of the financed counterparties and the relevance of such profiles within the financier's customer portfolio. Use of the sectorial/geographic approach must therefore be backed up by tools based on the single-name approach in contexts characterized by the considerable relevance of the specific risk.

Within the context of trade credit financing, an assessment of concentration risk through the approach based on sectorial/geographic characteristics seems suitable to prevent losses, leaving aside the motivation underlying the commercial credit application. From the perspective of the assessment of both the seller/assignor and trade debtor and given competition in the markets, repayment of debt is related to the placement of one's goods and/or services with end-purchasers. In that case, repayment of the exposure would seem to be prevailingly affected by trends in systemic variables, such as those related to sectorial markets, rather than by the counterparty's specific risk. Since trade credit has an anticyclical nature, the significance of the systemic variables is positively affected by the concentration of debtors in a sector and/or region and by the network effect among enterprises that arise from the extension of commercial credit (Cardoso-Lecourtois 2004).

Conclusions

Trade credits mitigate risk for lenders, even though the effectiveness requires a careful assessment of risk sources. Credit risk arises in default risk and dilution risk. Therefore, implementation of a credit risk system based on standard risk parameters requires previous adaptation of the relative framework, to evaluate both the risk of individual exposures and the portfolio exposure.

Default risk characterizes trade credit financing as it does other financial exposures, but trade credit financing allows financiers to enlarge the information set with observations from the procurement area that are not shared with other financiers. This provides the distinct opportunity to increase the quality of monitoring in terms of the breadth and timeliness of the information covered. Such information is critical in allowing the financier to distinguish between delinquencies and past dues signaling a default status, with the positive outcome of reducing counterparty misclassification. Moreover, such information is deemed useful to evaluate both the seller/assignor and the trade debtor, as well as the risk stemming from the combination of the counterparties. Dilution risk represents an ad hoc risk source in trade credit financing and has many potential causes that can be either ordinary, related to default risk, or operational risk oriented. Notwithstanding the multiplicity of causes, the negotiation of distinctive clauses and information capillarity allows the financier to distinguish among the different types of dilution and to properly manage them to limit future losses.

In the context of portfolio-level analysis, a concentration approach to assess future credit losses requires proper interpretation due to the financial exposure originating from a preexisting commercial relationship. In single-name approaches, the financier can report large exposures to the seller/assignor or the debtor purchasing the goods/services. The risk assessment must consider that the reimbursement of concentrated exposures is based on diversified sources and that payments are scheduled mainly in the short term. This requires previous investigation of the motivation of trade credit usage because concentrated exposures are associated with many invoices, on both the supplier and trade debtor sides, and they have only short-term maturity. Regarding the portfolio's sectorial/geographic characteristics, trade credit financial exposures can be more concentrated than other financial exposures. Therefore, careful analysis must uncover whether such concentration is associated with higher risk.

Conclusions

Trade credit is used extensively in both international and domestic transactions. Trade credit supports growth in low- and lower-middle-income countries, but its relevance is even stronger for developed countries, with an upward trend since the global financial crisis, driven by European countries exhibiting a stable pattern over time. Given the industry segmentation, the analysis of firm usage of trade credit reveals that larger firms are more comparable in the usage of trade credit and small and medium-sized firm dynamics are expected to be affected by local economic factors. The broadening of motivations for the usage of trade credit justifies the observed variability in the international data. Although traditional theories on the determinants of trade credit are confirmed over time, with empirical evidences on the substitution relationship strengthening the importance of financial motivations for constrained firms to smooth the negative effects of the bank credit cycle, the role for coordinating supply chains has become crucial, particularly since the global financial crisis, which has disclosed a more relationship-oriented approach to trade credit. As a matter of fact, trade credit flows perform as a key driver in the development of successful supply chains both at domestic and international level. Nonetheless, it is important to recognize that the market power of powerful firms and asymmetric credit contagion among the members, stemming from distressed trade debtors, pose potential concern in the fulfillment of the value maximization of the supply chain. The enrichment of the motivations for the usage of trade credit is accompanied by a diversification of domestic and international instruments to finance it, spanning from traditional to innovative financing solutions: Technology represents an enabling factor for the instruments analyzed, insofar as it increases the coverage of supply chain relationships and, therefore, the exploitation of the risk mitigation accompanying trade credit financing. Traditional self-liquidating loans still play a crucial role in enabling firms to discount invoices, but banks and financial intermediaries enrich pure financing services by allowing firms to outsource completely all needs connected with the management of trade receivables, as in the case of factoring. A potential alternative in international transactions is represented by letter of credit and guarantees, even though open account transactions are increasing over time consistently with the increasing importance of supply chain finance services: Such instruments are based on a combination of existing and new products created by means of technological applications, as in the case of bank payment obligations. Among market instruments, commercial papers still represent a core financing solution, but the issuer quality requirements have pushed downward the growth of the market for asset-backed commercial papers, which is still recovering after a strong downturn since the global financial crisis. The application of technology to market instruments enables the funding of invoices also by noninstitutional investors and, therefore, discloses a new asset class for retail investors that happens to be one of the most promising options in peer-to-peer lending. Nonetheless, this is to underline that in finance instruments differentiated legal and operational features still matter for both bank and market instruments, along with relevant effects on the effectiveness of risk mitigation for financiers, regardless of the kind of managing approach used for dealing with existing and future trade credits.

Trade credit is able to mitigate the financiers' exposure to credit risks. Default risk characterizes trade credit financing, as it does in other financial exposures, but trade credit financing also allows financiers to enlarge their information set with observations on the procurement area that reveal unique characteristics and information that is not shared with other types of financiers. At the individual exposure level, available information is critical in allowing the financier to distinguish between delinquencies and defaults, whereas a careful portfolio analysis uncovers whether concentrated exposures both at name or geographical/sectional level are associated with higher risk. Considering dilution risk, notwithstanding the multiplicity of causes, the negotiation of distinct contractual clauses and the capillarity of the information allow financiers to distinguish among the different types of dilution, also with respect to default risk, and properly manage them to limit future losses and improve the performance of operational processes. Ultimately, a credit risk management system can help financiers to extract value from the ample and updated proprietary set of information by organizing it consistently for exploitation by the financier or third parties.

References

Abad, P. L., and C. Jaggi. 2003. "A Joint Approach for Setting Unit Price and the Length of the Credit Period for a Seller When End Demand is Price Sensitive." *International Journal of Production Economics* 83, no. 2, pp. 115–22.

Abuzayed, B. 2012. "Working Capital Management and Firms' Performance in Emerging Markets: The Case of Jordan." *International Journal of Managerial Finance* 8, no. 2, pp. 155–79.

Adrian, T., K. Kimbrough, and D. Marchioni. May 2011. "The Federal Reserve's Commercial Paper Funding Facility." *Federal Reserve Bank of New York Economic Policy Review.*

Alan, Y., and V. Gaur. 2012. "Operational Investment and Capital Structure Under Asset Based Lending: A One Period Model." Working Paper, Cornell University, Ithaca, NY.

Alworth, J., and C. Borio. 1993. "Commercial Paper Markets: A Survey." BIS Economic Papers, No. 37. Bank for International Settlements, Basel.

Altman, E. 1984. "A Further Investigation on the Bankruptcy Cost Question." *Journal of Finance* 39, no. 4, pp. 1067–89.

Altman, E., and A. Saunders. 1998. "Credit Risk Measurement: Developments over the Last 20 Years." *Journal of Banking and Finance* 21, no. 11–12, pp. 1721–42.

Altman, E., and P. Narayanan. 1997. "An International Survey of Business Failure Classification Models." *Financial Markets, Institutions and Instruments* 6, no. 2, pp. 1–97.

Amiti, M., and D. Weinstein. 2011. "Exports and Financial Shocks." *Quarterly Journal of Economics* 126, no. 4, pp. 1841–77.

Arshinder, A., and S. Deshmukh. 2008. "Supply Chain Coordination: Perspectives, Empirical Studies and Research Directions." *International Journal of Production Economics* 115, no. 5, pp. 316–335.

Asmundson, I., T. Dorsey, A. Khachatryan, I. Niculcea, and M. Saito. 2011. "Trade and Trade Finance in the 2008-09 Financial Crisis." IMF Working Papers, No. 1116. Washington, DC: International Monetary Fund.

Assifact. 2012. *Database delle abitudini di pagamento, Guida operativa.* Milan: Assifact.

Aktas, N., E. De Bodt, F. Lobez, and J. Statnik. 2012. "The Information Content of Trade Credit." *Journal of Banking and Finance* 36, no. 5, pp. 1402–13.

Atanasova, C. 2007. "Access to Institutional Finance and the Use of Trade Credit." *Financial Management* 36, no. 1, pp. 49–67.

Atanasova, C. 2012. "How Do Firms Choose Between Intermediary and Supplier Finance?" *Financial Management* 41, no. 1, pp. 207–28.

Auboin, M., and M. Engemann. 2014. "Testing the Trade Credit Link: Evidence from Data on Export Credit Insurance." *Review of World Economics* 150, no. 4, pp. 715–43.

Barrot, J. 2016. "Trade Credit and Industry Dynamics: Evidence from Trucking Firms." *Journal of Finance* 71, no. 5, pp. 1975–2015.

Basel Committee on Banking Supervision. 2004. *International Convergence of Capital Measurement and Capital Standards.* Basel: Basel Committee on Banking Supervision.

Basel Committee on Banking Supervision. 2006. *International Convergence of Capital Measurement and Capital Standards, A Revised Framework.* Basel: Basel Committee on Banking Supervision.

Bastos, R., and J. Pindado. 2013. "Trade Credit during a Financial Crisis: A Panel Data Analysis." *Journal of Business Research* 66, no. 5, pp. 614–20.

Bate, S., S. Bushweller, and E. Rutan. 2002. "The Fundamentals of Asset Backed Commercial Paper." Special Report, Moody's Investors Service, New York, NY.

Battiston, S., D. Delli Gatti, M. Gallegati, B. Greewald, and J. Stiglitz. 2007. "Credit Chains and Bankruptcy Propagation in Production Networks." *Journal of Economic Dynamics & Control* 31, no. 6, pp. 2061–84.

Beaver, W. 1966. "Financial Ratios as Predictors of Failure." *Journal of Accounting Research* 4, pp. 71–111.

Beck, T., A. Demirgüç-Kunt, and V. Maksimovic. 2003. "Bank Competition, Financing Obstacles and Access to Credit." World Bank Policy Research Working Paper, No. 2996. World Bank, Washington, DC.

Beck, T., A. Demirgüç-Kunt, and V. Maksimovic. 2008. "Financing Patterns around the World: Are Small Firms Different?" *Journal of Financial Economics* 89, no. 3, pp. 467–87.

Berger, A. N., and G. F. Udell. 1998. "The Economics of Small Business Finance: The Roles of Private Equity and Debts Markets in the Financial Growth Cycle." *Journal of Banking and Finance* 22, no. 6, pp. 613–73.

Berlin, P. 2003. "Trade Credit: Why Do Production Firms Act as Financial Intermediaries?" *Business Review*, Third quarter, pp. 21–28.

Berne Union. 2016. *Yearbook 2016.* London, UK: Berne Union.

Bessis, J. 2015. *Risk Management in Banking.* Hoboken: Wiley.

Biais, B., and C. Gollier. 1997. "Trade Credit and Credit Rationing." *Review of Financial Studies* 10, no. 4, pp. 903–38.

Bigelli, M., and J. Sánchez-Vidal. 2012. "Cash Holdings in Private Firms." *Journal of Banking & Finance* 36, no. 1, pp. 26–35.

Blazenko, G., and K. Vandezande. 2003. "The Product Differentiation Hypothesis for Corporate Trade Credit." *Managerial and Decision Economics* 24, no. 6–7, pp. 457–69.

Boissay, F., and R. Gropp. 2013. "Payment Defaults and Interfirm Liquidity Provision." *Review of Finance* 17, no. 6, pp. 1853–94.

Boot, A. 2000. "Relationship Banking: What We Know?" *Journal of Financial Intermediation* 9, no. 1, pp. 7–25.

Borello, G., V. De Crescenzo, and F. Pichler. 2014. "Le piattaforme di Financial Return crowdfunding nell'Unione Europea." *Bancaria* 70, no. 12, pp. 77–90.

Bottazzi, G., M. Grazzi, A. Secchi, and F. Tamagni. 2011. "Financial and Economic Determinants of Firm Default." *Journal of Evolutionary Economics* 21, no. 3, pp. 373–406.

Bougheas, S., S. Mateut, and P. Mizen. 2009. "Corporate Trade Credit and Inventories: New Evidence of a Trade-off from Accounts Payable and Receivable." *Journal of Banking and Finance* 33, no. 2, pp. 300–7.

Brennan, M., V. Miksimovic, and J. Zechner. 1988. "Vendor Financing." *Journal of Finance* 43, no. 5, pp. 1127–41.

Breza, E., and A. Liberman. 2017. "Financial Contracting and Organizational Form: Evidence from the Regulation of Trade Credit." *Journal of Finance* 72, no. 1, pp. 291–324.

Bris, A., and I. Welch. 2005. "The Optimal Concentration of Creditors." *Journal of Finance* 60, no. 5, pp. 2194–212.

Bukart, M., and T. Ellingsen. 2004. "In-Kind Finance: A Theory of Trade." *American Economic Review* 94, no. 3, pp. 569–90.

Cachon, G. 2003. "Supply Chain Coordination with Contracts." In *Handbooks in Operations Research and Management Science,* eds. A. De Kok and S. Graves. Amsterdam: Elsevier.

Cachon, G. 2004. "The Allocation of Inventory Risk in a Supply Chain: Push, Pull, and Advance-Purchase Discount Contracts." *Management Science* 50, no. 2, pp. 222–38.

Calamoris, C. 1989. "The Motivations for Loan Commitments Backing Commercial Paper: A Comment on 'Commercial Paper, Bank Reserve Requirements, and the Informational Role of Loan Commitments." *Journal of Banking and Finance* 13, no. 2, pp. 271–77.

Calamoris, C., C. Himmelberg, and P. Wachtel. 1995. "Commercial Paper, Corporate Finance, and the Business Cycle: A Microeconomic Perspective." *Carnegie-Rochester Conference Series on Public Policy* 42, pp. 203–50.

Carbo Valverde, S., F. Rodriguez Fernandez, and G. Udell. 2016. "Trade Credit, The Financial Crises and SME Access to Finance." *Journal of Money, Credit and Banking* 48, no. 1, pp. 113–43.

Cardoso-Lecourtois, M. 2004. "Chain Reactions, Trade Credit and the Business Cycle." Econometric Society North American Summer Meetings, No. 331.

Carignani, A., and V. Gemmo. 2007. "Prestiti Peer to Peer: Modelli di business e strategie." *Credito popolare* 14, no. 3–4, pp. 409–25.

Carling, K., and S. Lundberg. 2002. "Bank Lending, Geographical Distance and Credit Risk: An Empirical Assessment of the Church Tower Principle." Sveriges Riksbank Working Paper Series, No. 144. Stockholm, Sweden: Sveriges Riksbank.

Cerasi, V., and S. Daltung. 2000. "The Optimal Size of Bank: Costs and Benefits of Diversification." *European Economic Review* 44, no. 9, pp. 1701–26.

Cheng X., and A. Wang. 2012. "Trade Credit Contract with Limited Liability in the Supply Chain with Budget Constraints." *Annals of Operations Research* 196, no. 1, pp. 153–65.

Chernobai, A., S. Rachev, and F. Fabozzi. 2007. *Operational Risk: A Guide to Basel II Capital Requirements, Models, and Analysis*. Hoboken: Wiley.

Chung, K. 1990. "Inventory Decision under Demand Uncertainty: A Contingent Claims Approach." *Financial Review* 25, no. 4, pp. 623–40.

Cook, L. 1999. "Trade Credit and Bank Finance: Financing Small Firms in Russia." *Journal of Business Venturing* 14, no. 5–6, pp. 493–518.

Committee on the Global Financial System. 2014. "Trade Finance: Developments and Issues." CGFS Papers, No. 50. Bank for International Settlements, Basel.

Connell, W. 2014. "The Economic Impact of Late Payments." Economic Papers, No. 531. Brussels.

Coricelli, F. 1996. "Finance and Growth in Economies in Transition." *European Economic Review* 40, no. 3–4, pp. 645–53.

Coulibaly, B., H. Sapriza, and A. Zlate. 2013. "Financial Frictions, Trade Credit, and the 2008–09 Global Financial Crisis." *International* Review *of Economics and Finance* 26, pp. 25–38.

Covitz, D., Liang N., and G. Suarez. 2013. "The Evolution of a Financial Crisis: Collapse of the Asset-Backed Commercial Paper Market". *Journal of Finance* 68, no.3, pp. 815–48.

Crook, J., D. Eldman, and L. Thomas. 2007. "Recent Developments in Consumer Credit Risk Assessment." *European Journal of Operational Research* 183, no. 3, pp. 1447–65.

Crook, R., and J. Combs. 2007. "Sources and Consequences of Bargaining Power in Supply Chains." *Journal of Operations Management* 25, no. 2, pp. 546–55.

Cull, R., L. Xu, and T. Zhu. 2009. "Formal Finance and Trade Credit during China's Transition." *Journal of Financial Intermediation* 18, no. 2, pp. 173–92.

Cunāt, V. 2007. "Trade Credit: Suppliers as Debt Collectors and Insurance Providers." *Review of Financial Studies* 20, no. 2, pp. 491–527.

Dallocchio, M., and A. Salvi. 2004. *Finanza Aziendale.* Milano: Egea.

Danielsson, J., B. Jorgensen, and C. de Vreis. 2002. "Incentives for Effective Risk Management." *Journal of Banking and Finance* 26, no. 7, pp. 1407–25.

Dass, N., J. Kale, and V. Nanda. 2015. "Trade Credit, Relationship Specific Investment and Product Market Power." *Review of Finance* 19, no. 5, pp. 1867–923.

Degryse, H., L. Lu, and S. Ongena. 2016. "Informal or Formal Financing? Evidence on the Co-funding of Chinese Firms." *Journal of Financial Intermediation* 27, pp. 31–50.

De Laurentis, G. 2001. *Rating interni e credit risk management.* Rome: Bancaria Editrice.

De Laurentis, G., D. Quatraro, and L. Santambrogio. 2017. "Il rischio di name concentration è sopravvalutato e può ridurre redditività e qualità delle relazioni banca-impresa." *Bancaria,* No. 7–8.

Demirguc-Kunt, A., and V. Maksimovic. 2001. "Firms as Financial Intermediaries, Evidence from Trade Credit Data." World Bank Policy Research Paper, No. 2696. World Bank, Washington, DC.

Deng, S., and E. Elyasiani. 2008. "Geographic Diversification, Bank Holding Company Value, and Risk." *Journal of Money, Credit and Banking* 40, no. 6, pp. 1217–38.

DeSimone, J., and V. Moscowitz. 2004 January. "U.S. Trade Receivables Securitization: Offset Risk Under Long-Term Contracts." Standard and Poor's Editor's Note, New York, NY.

Dietch, M., and J. Petey. 2004. "Should SME Exposures be Treated as Retail or Corporate Exposures? A Comparative Analysis of Default Probabilities and ASSET CORRELATIONS in French and German SMEs." *Journal of Banking and Finance* 28, no. 4, pp. 773–88.

Direr, A. 2001. "Trade Credit and Systemic Risk." *Recherches Economiques de Louvain* 68, no. 3, pp. 371–84.

Du, R., A. Banarjiee, and S. Kim. 2013. "Coordination of Two-echelon Supply Chains Using Wholesale Price Discount and Credit Option." *International Journal of Production Economics* 143, no. 2, pp. 327–34.

El Ghoul, S., and X. Zheng. 2016. "Trade Credit Provision and National Culture." *Journal of Corporate Finance* 41, pp. 475–501.

Emery, G. W. 1984. "A Pure Financial Explanation for Trade Credit." *Journal of Financial and Quantitative Analysis* 19, no. 3, pp. 271–85.

Emery, G. W. 1987. "An Optimal Financial Response to Variable Demand." *Journal of Financial and Quantitative Analysis* 22, no. 2, pp. 209–25.

Eun, C., and B. Rensik. 2018. *International Financial Management*. New York, NY: McGraw Hill.

Everett, C. 2014. "Origins and Development of Credit-Based Crowd funding." *SSRN Electronic Journal*, p. 30. doi:10.2139/ssrn.2442897.

Faith, R. L., and R. D. Tollison. 1981. "Contractual Exchange and the Timing of Payment." *Journal of Economic Behavior and Organization* 1, no. 4, pp. 325–42.

Fabbri, D., and A. Menichini. 2010. "Trade Credit, Collateral Liquidation, and Borrowing Constraints." *Journal of Financial Economics* 96, no. 3, pp. 413–32.

Ferrando, A., and K. Mulier. 2013. "Do Firms Use the Trade Credit Channel to Manage Growth?" *Journal of Banking and Finance* 37, no. 8, pp. 3035–46.

Ferris, J. S. 1981. "A Transactions Theory of Trade Credit Use." *Quarterly Journal of Economics* 96, no. 2, pp. 243–70.

Fisman R. 2001. "Trade Credit and Productive Efficiency in Developing Countries." *World Development* 29, no. 2, pp. 311–21.

Fisman, R., and I. Love. 2003. "Trade Credit, Financial Intermediary Development, and Industry Growth." *Journal of Finance* 58, no. 1, pp. 353–74.

Fitzpatrick, A., and B. Lien. 2013. "The Use of Trade Credit by Businesses." *Reserve Bank of Australia Bulletin*, September Quarter, No. 9.

Florentsen, B., M. Møller, and N. C. Nielsen. 2003. "Reimbursement of VAT on Written-Off Receivables." *International Tax Journal* no. 4, pp. 43–64.

Frank, M., and V. Maksimovic. 2004. "Trade Credit, Collateral and Adverse Selection." *SSRN Electronic Journal*, p. 41. doi:10.2139/ssrn.87868.

Gan, X., S. Sethi, and H. Yan. 2004. "Coordination of Supply Chains with Risk-Averse Agents." *Productions and Operations Management* 13, no. 2, pp. 135–49.

Garcia-Appendini, E., and J. Montoriol-Garriga. 2013. "Firms as Liquidity Providers: Evidence from the 2007–2008 Financial Crisis." *Journal of Financial Economics* 109, no. 1, pp. 272–91.

Garvin, L. 1996. "Credit, Information, and Trust in the Law of Sales: The Credit Seller's Right of Reclamation." *UCLA Law Review* 44, pp. 247–350.

Ge, Y., and J. Qiu. 2007. "Financial Development, Bank Discrimination and Trade Credit." *Journal of Banking and Finance* 31, no. 2, pp. 513–30.

Giesecke, K., and S. Weber. 2006. "Credit Contagion and Aggregate Losses." *Journal of Economic Dynamics and Control* 30, no. 5, pp. 741–67.

Giannetti, M., M. Burkart, and T. Ellingsten. 2011. "What You Sell Is What You Lend? Explaining Trade Credit Contracts." *Review of Financial Studies* 24, no. 4, pp. 1261–98.

Gibilaro, L. 2004. "Il trattamento dei crediti commerciali nel Nuovo Accordo sul Capitale." *Banche e Banchieri* 31, no. 4, pp. 308–20.

Gibilaro, L. 2006. "L'impatto del Nuovo Accordo sul Capitale sulla standardizzazione dei processi del risk management: il rischio di dilution." AA.VV. eds, in *I processi di standardizzazione in azienda, Aspetti istituzionali, organizzativi, manageriali, finanziari e contabili, Atti del X Convegno nazionale di Aidea Giovani Dipartimento di Studi Aziendali Università degli studi di Napoli Parthenope 17-18 marzo 2005*, ed. AA.VV. Rome: Franco Angeli.

Gibilaro, L., and G. Mattarocci. 2010. "Predictors of Net Trade Credit Exposure: Evidence from the Italian Market." *International Journal of Business and Finance Research* 4, no. 4, pp. 103–19.

Giesecke, K., and S. Weber. 2004. "Cyclical Correlations, Credit Contagion and Portfolio Losses." *Journal of Banking and Finance* 28, no. 12, pp. 3009–36.

Gordy, M. B. 2003. "A Risk Factor Model Foundation for Ratings-Based Bank Capital Rules." *Journal of Financial Intermediation* 12, no. 3, pp. 199–232.

Guariglia, A., and S. Mateut. 2006. "Credit Channel, Trade Credit Channel, and Inventory Investment: Evidence from a Panel of UK Firms." *Journal of Banking and Finance* 30, no. 10, pp. 2835–56.

Guiso, L., P. Sapienza, and L. Zingales. 2013. "The Determinants of Attitudes toward Strategic Default on Mortgages." *Journal of Finance* 68, no. 4, pp. 1473–515.

Ha, A., Q. Tian, and S. Tong. 2017. "Information Sharing in Competing Supply Chains with Production Cost Reduction." *Manufacturing & Service Operations Management* 19, no. 2, pp. 246–62.

Hahn, T. 1998. "Commercial Paper." In *Instruments of the Money Market*, eds. T. Cook and R. Laroche. Richmond, VA: Federal Reserve Bank of Richmond.

Han, X., Wang, X., and H. Wang. 2012. "The inter-enterprise relationship and trade credit", *Nankai Business Review International* 4, no. 1, pp. 49–65

Hanson, S., N. H. Pesaran, and T. Schuerman. 2005. "Scope of Credit Risk Diversification." IEPR Working Paper, No. 18. Institute of Economic Policy Research (IEPR).

He, M., C. Ren, B. Shao, Q. Wang, and J. Dong. 2010. "Financial Supply Chain Management." In *Proceedings of the IEEE Conference*. Red Hook, NY: Curran Associates.

Heitfield, E., S. Burton, and S. Chomsisengphet. 2005. "Risk Sensitive Regulatory Capital Rules for Hedged Credit Exposures." In *Counterparty Credit Risk Modelling: Pricing, Risk Management and Regulation*, ed. M. Pykhtin. London, UK: Risk Waters Group.

Hernando, J. R. 2016. "Crowdfunding: The Collaborative Economy for Channelling Institutional and Household Savings." *Research in International Business and Finance* 38, pp. 326–37.

Hertzel, M. G., Z. Li, M. Officer, and K. Rodgers. 2008. "Inter-firm Linkages and the Wealth Effects of Financial Distress along the Supply Chain." *Journal of Financial Economics* 87, no. 2, pp. 374–87.

Hofmann, E., and H. Kotzab. 2010. "A Supply Chain-Oriented Approach of Working Capital Management." *Journal of Business Logistics* 31, no. 2, pp. 305–30.

Howorth, C., and P. Westhead. 2003. "The Focus of Working Capital Management in UK Small Firms." *Management Accounting Research* 14, no. 2, pp. 94–111.

Hyndman, K., and G. Serio. 2010. "Competition and Inter-firm Credit: Theory and Evidence from Firm-level Data in Indonesia." *Journal of Development Economics* 93, no. 1, pp. 88–108.

Huang, H., X. Shi, and S. Zhang. 2011. "Counter-cyclical Substitution between Trade Credit and Bank Credit." *Journal of Banking and Finance* 35, no. 8, pp. 1859–78.

Huyghebaert, N. 2006. "On the Determinants and Dynamics of Trade Credit Use: Empirical Evidence from Business Start-ups." *Journal of Business Finance & Accounting* 33, no. 1–2, pp. 305–28.

International Chamber of Commerce. 2013. *Uniform Rules for Bank Payment Obligations*. Paris: ICC Services.

International Chamber of Commerce. 2016. *2016 Rethinking Trade and Finance*. Paris: ICC Services.

International Chamber of Commerce. 2017. *2017 Rethinking Trade and Finance*. Paris: ICC Services.

International Monetary Fund (IMF), Bankers Association for Finance and Trade and International Financial Services Association (BAFT-IFSTA). 2010. *A Survey among Banks Assessing the Current Trade Finance Environment, Trade Finance Services: Current Environment and Recommendations: Wave 3*. Washington, DC: IMF, BAFT-IFSTA.

International Monetary Fund (IMF), Bankers Association for Finance and Trade and International Financial Services Association (BAFT-IFSTA). 2011. *6th Trade Finance Survey*. Washington, DC: IMF, BAFT-IFSTA.

Ivashina, V., and D. Scharfstein. 2010. "Bank Lending during the Financial Crisis of 2008." *Journal of Financial Economics* 97, no. 3, pp. 319–38.

Jaber, M., and I. Osman. 2006. "Coordinating a Two-level Supply Chain with Delay in Payments and Profit Sharing." *Computers & Industrial Engineering* 50, no. 4, pp. 385–400.

Jaffee, D. M., and J. E. Stiglitz. 1990. "Credit Rationing." In *Handbook of Monetary Economics,* eds. B. M. Friedman, and F. H. Hahn. Amsterdam: North Holland.

Jacobson, T., and E. Von Schevdin. 2015. "Trade Credit and the Propagation of Corporate Failure: An Empirical Analysis." *Econometrica* 83, no. 4, pp. 1315–71.

Jain, N. 2001. "Monitoring Costs and Trade Credit." *Quarterly Review of Economics and Finance* 41, no. 1, pp. 89–110.

Jones, S., and R. Walker. 2007. "Explanators of Local Government Distress." *Abacus* 43, no. 3, pp. 396–418.

Jorion, P., and G. Zhang. 2009. "Credit Contagion from Counterparty Risk". *Journal of Finance*, 64, no. 5, pp. 2053–87.

Katz, A., and J. Blatt. 2008. "Funding through the Use of Trade Receivable Securitizations." In *The Handbook of Finance*, ed. F. Fabozzi. Hoboken: John Wiley and Sons.

Kamp, A., A. Pfingsten, and D. Porath. 2005. "Do Banks Diversify Loan Portfolios? A Tentative Answer Based on Individual Bank Loan Portfolios." Deutsche Bundesbank Discussion Paper, No. 3. Deutsche Bundesbank, Frankfurt am Main.

Kiyotaki, N., and J. Moore. 1997. *Credit Chains*. Mimeo: London School of Economics.

Klapper, L. 2006. "The Role of Factoring for Financing Small and Medium Enterprises." *Journal of Banking and Finance* 30, no. 11, pp. 3111–30.

Klapper, L., L. Laeven, and R. Rajan. 2012. "Trade Credit Contracts." *Review of Financial Studies* 25, no. 3, pp. 838–67.

Kouvelis, P., and W. Zhao. 2012. "Financing the Newsvendor: Supplier vs. Bank, and the Structure of Optimal Trade Credit Contracts." *Operations Research* 60, no. 3, pp. 566–80.

Kozak, S. 2015. "Concentration of Credit Exposure as a Significant Source of Risk in Banking Activities: The Idea and Methods of Estimation." *eFinanse* 11, no. 3, pp. 103–15.

Laffer, A. 1970. "Trade Credit and the Money Market." *Journal of Political Economy* 78, no. 2, pp. 239–67.

Lai, G., L. G. Debo, and K. Sycara. 2009. "Sharing Inventory Risk in Supply Chain: The Implication of Financial Constraint." *Omega* 37, no. 4, pp. 811–25.

Lambert, D., M. Cooper, and J. Pagh. 1998. "Supply Chain Management: Implementation Issues and Research Opportunities." *International Journal of Logistic Management* 9, no. 2, pp. 1–19.

Lee, Y. W., and J. D. Stowe. 1993. "Product Risk, Asymmetric Information, and Trade Credit." *Journal of Financial and Quantitative Analysis* 28, no. 2, pp. 285–300.

Lee, C. H., and B. D. Rhee. 2011. "Trade Credit for Supply Chain Coordination." *European Journal of Operational Research* 214, pp. 136–46.

Lewellen, W. G., J. J. McConnel, and J. A. Scott. 1980. "Capital Market Influence on Trade Credit Policy." *Journal of Financial Research* 3, no. 1, pp. 105–13.

Li, D., Y. Lu, T. Ng, and J. Yang. 2016. "Does Trade Credit Boost Firm Performance?" *Economic Development and Cultural Change* 64, no. 3, pp. 573–602.

Li, X., and Q. Wang. 2007. "Coordination Mechanisms of Supply Chain Systems." *European Journal of Operational Research* 179, pp. 1–16.

Long, M., I. Malitz, and S. Ravid. 1993. "Trade Credit, Quality Guarantees, and Product Marketability." *Financial Management* 22, no. 4, pp. 117–27.

Longhofer, S. D., and J. A. Santos. 2000. "The Importance of Bank Seniority for Relationship Lending." *Journal of Financial Intermediation* 9, no. 1, pp. 57–89.

Love, I., L. Preve, and V. Allende. 2007. "Trade Credit and Bank Credit: Evidence from Recent Financial Crises." *Journal of Financial Economics* 83, no. 2, pp. 453–69.

Love, I., and R. Zaidi. 2010. "Trade Credit, Bank Credit and Financial Crisis." *International Review of Finance* 10, no. 1, pp. 125–47.

Luo, J. 2007. "Buyer-vendor Inventory Coordination with Credit Period Incentives." *International Journal of Production Economics* 108, no. 1–2, pp. 143–52.

Luo, J., and Q. Zhang. 2012. "Trade Credit: A New Mechanism to Coordinate Supply Chain." *Operations Research Letters* 40, no. 5, pp. 378–84.

Mach, T. 2014. "Business to Business Credit to Small Firms." *Finance and Economics Discussion Series,* no. 55. Washington, DC: Federal Reserve Bank.

Mateut, S., Bougheas, S., and P. Mizen. 2006. "Trade Credit, Bank Lending and monetary policy transmission". *European Economic Review* 50, pp. 603–29.

Mateut, S. 2014. "Reverse Trade Credit or Default Risk? Explaining the Use of Prepayments by Firms." *Journal of Corporate Finance* 29, pp. 303–26.

McMillan, J., and C. Woodruff. 1999. "Interfirm Relationships and Informal Credit in Vietnam." *Quarterly Journal of Economics* 114, no. 4, pp. 1285–320.

McMillan, J., and C. Woodruff. 2002. "The Central Role of Entrepreneurs in Transition Economies." *Journal of Economic Perspectives* 16, no. 3, pp. 153–70.

Meijer, C., and M. Menon. 2012. "Bank Payment Obligation: The Missing Link?" *Journal of Payments Strategy and Systems* 6, no. 3, pp. 232–45.

Meltzer, A. H. 1960. "Mercantile Credit, Monetary Policy, and Size of Firms." *Review of Economics and Statistics* 42, no. 4, pp. 429–37.

Menichini, A. 2011. "Inter-firm Trade Finance in Times of Crisis." *World Economy* 34, no. 10, pp. 1788–808.

Messmacher, M. 2001. "The Relationship between Trade Credit and Investment in Mexico: 1998–2000." Conference on Financial Markets in Mexico Organized by the Center for Research on Economic Development and Policy Reform at Stanford University, October 5–6, 2001.

Mian, S. L., and C. W. Smith. 1992. "Accounts Receivable Management Policy: Theory and Evidence." *Journal of Finance* 47, no. 1, pp. 169–200.

Myers, S. C., and R. Rajan. 1998. "The Paradox of Liquidity." *Quarterly Journal of Economics* 113, no. 3, pp. 733–71.

Molina, C., and L. Preve. 2012. "An Empirical Analysis of the Effect of Financial Distress on Trade Credit." *Financial Management* 41, pp. 187–205.

Modasky, R. A., and J. Massimino. 2011. "Asset-Based Financing Basics." *Journal of Accountancy* 212, no. 2, pp. 41–44.

Morse, A. 2015. "Peer to Peer Crowdfunding: Information and the Potential for Disruption in Consumer Lending." NBER Working Paper, No. 20899. Cambridge: National Bureau of Economic Research.

Munoz, M., L. Norden, and S. Van Kampen. 2016. "Substitution Effects in Private Debt: Evidence from SMEs." *SSRN Electronic Journal,* p. 51. doi:10.2139/ssrn.2578291.

Murfin, J., and K. Njoroge. 2015. "The Implicit Costs of Trade Credit Borrowing by Large Firms." *Review of Financial Studies* 28, no. 1, pp. 112–45.

Murphy, D. 2008. *Understanding Risk: The Theory and Practice of Financial Risk Management,* Danvers: CRC Press.

Nadiri, M. 1969. "The Determinants of Trade Credit in the U.S. Total Manufacturing Sector." *Econometrica* 37, no. 3, pp. 408–23.

Ng, C. K., J. K. Smith, and R. L. Smith. 1999. "Evidence on the Determinants of Credit Terms Used in Interfirm Trade." *Journal of Finance* 54, no. 3, pp. 1109–29.

Nielsen, J. H. 2002. "Trade Credit and the Bank Lending Channel." *Journal of Money, Credit and Banking* 34, no. 1, pp. 226–53.

OECD. 2015. *New Approaches to SME and Entrepreneurship Financing: Broadening the Range of Instruments.* Paris: OECD Publishing.

Omiccioli, M. 2005. "Il credito commerciale: fatti, problemi e teorie." In *Imprese o intermediari? Aspetti finanziari e commerciali del credito tra imprese in Italia,* eds. L. Cannari, S. Chiri, and M. Omiccioli. Bologna: Il Mulino.

Paul, S., and N. Wilson. 2006. "Trade Credit Supply: An Empirical Investigation of Companies Level Data." *Journal of Accounting, Business and Management* 13, no. 10, pp. 85–113.

Petersen, M., and R. Rajan. 1997. "Trade Credit: Theories and Evidence." *Review of Financial Studies* 10, no. 3, pp. 661–91.

Pfhol, H., and M. Gomm. 2009. "Supply Chain Finance: Optimizing Financial Flows in Supply Chains." *Logistic Research* 1, no. 3, pp. 149–61.

Pilcer, S. 1996. "Trade Receivables Update: Concentrating on Dilution—Focus on Capital Goods and Consumer Products Receivables." *Special Report, Moody's Investor Services,* January, New York, NY.

Pike, R., N. Cheng, K. Cravens, and D. Lamminmaki. 2005. "Trade Credit Terms: Asymmetric Information and Price Discrimination Evidence from Three Continents." *Journal of Business Finance & Accounting* 32, no. 5–6, pp. 1197–233.

Raddatz, C. 2010. "Credit Chains and Sectoral Comovement: Does the Use of Trade Credit Amplify Sectoral Shocks?" *Review of Economics and Statistics* 92, no. 4, pp. 985–1003.

Rajan, R., and L. Zingales. 1995. "What do We Know about Capital Structure? Some Evidence from International Data." *Journal of Finance* 50, no. 5, pp. 1421–60.

Resti, A., and A. Sironi. 2007. *Risk Management and Shareholders' Value in Banking: From Risk Measurement Models to Capital Allocation Policies.* Hoboken: Wiley and Sons.

Robin, R. 2011. *International Corporate Finance.* New York, NY: McGraw Hill.

Santella, P. 2005. "Il costo dei rimedi giuridici del credito commerciale." In *Imprese o intermediari? Aspetti finanziari e commerciali del credito tra imprese in Italia*, eds. L. Cannari, S. Chiri, and M. Omiccioli. Bologna: Il Mulino.

Santomero, A. N. 1997. "Commercial Banking Risk Management: An Analysis of the Process." *Journal of Financial Service Research* 12, no. 2–3, pp. 83–115.

Sarmah, S., D. Acharya, and S. Goyal. 2008. "Coordination of a Single-manufacturer/Multi-buyer Supply Chain with Credit Option." *International Journal of Production Economics* 111, no. 2, pp. 676–85.

Schiff, M., and Z. Lieber. 1974. "A Model for the Integration of Credit and Inventory Management." *Journal of Finance* 29, no. 1, pp. 133–40.

Schwartz, R. A. 1974. "An Economic Model of Trade Credit." *Journal of Financial & Quantitative Analysis* 9, no. 3, pp. 643–57.

Schwartz, R. A., and D. Whitcomb. 1979. "The Trade Credit Decision" In *Handbook of Financial Economics*, eds. L. James and L. Bicksler. Amsterdam: North-Holland.

Seifert, D. and R. Seifert. 2007. "Financing the Chain." *International Commerce Review* 10, no. 1, pp. 33–44.

Seifert, D., R. Seifert, and M. Protopappa-Sieke. 2013. "A Review of Trade Credit Literature: Opportunities for Research in Operations." *European Journal of Operational Research* 231, no. 2, pp. 245–56.

Smith, J. K. 1987. "Trade Credit and Information Asymmetry." *Journal of Finance* 42, no. 4, pp. 863–72.

Stevens, G. C. 1989. "Integrating the Supply Chain." *International Journal of Physical Distribution & Materials Management* 19, no. 8, pp. 3–8.

Stomper, A. 2006. "A Theory of Banks' Industry Expertise, Market Power and Credit Risk." *Management Science* 52, no. 10, pp. 1618–33.

Sugirin, M. 2009. "Financial Supply Chain Management." *Journal of Corporate Treasury Management* 2, no. 3, pp. 237–40.

Summer, B., and N. Wilson. 2002. "An Empirical Investigation of Trade Credit Demand." *International Journal of the Economics and Business* 9, no. 2, pp. 257–70.

Summers, B., and N. Wilson. 2003. "Trade Credit and Customer Relationships." *Managerial and Decision Economics* 24, no. 6–7, pp. 439–55.

Swift. September 2015. "A New Start for Supply Chain Finance." *White Paper*.

Tang, T., and L. Chi. 2005. "Predicting Multilateral Trade Credit Risks: Comparisons of Logit and Fuzzy Logic Models using ROC Curve Analysis." *Expert Systems with Applications* 28, no. 3, pp. 547–56.

Teruel, P., and P. Solano. 2010. "Determinants of Trade Credit: A Comparative Study of European SME." *International Small Business Journal* 28, no. 3, pp. 215–33.

Titman, S., and R. Wessels. 1988. "The Determinants of Capital Structure." *Journal of Finance* 43, no. 1, pp. 1–40.

Tsuruta, D. 2013. "Credit Contagion and Trade Credit: Evidence from Small Business Data in Japan." *Asian Economic Journal* 27, no. 4, pp. 341–67.

Uchida, H., G. Udell, and W. Watanabe. 2013. "Are Trade Creditors Relationship Lenders?" *Japan and the World Economy* 25–26, January–March, pp. 24–38.

Ulku, S., L. Toktay, and E. Yucesan. 2007. "Risk Ownership in Contract Manufacturing." *Manufacturing Service Operations Management* 9, no. 3, pp. 225–41.

Van der Vliet, K., M. J. Reindorp, and J. C. Fransoo. 2015. "The Price of Reverse Factoring: Financing Rates vs Payment Delays." *European Journal of Operational Research* 242, no. 3, pp. 842–53.

Voordeckers, W., and T. Steijvers. 2006. "Business Collateral and Personal Commitments in SME Lending." *Journal of Banking and Finance* 30, no. 11, pp. 3067–86.

Wagner, S., C. Bode, and P. Koziol. 2008. "Supplier Default Dependencies: Empirical Evidence from the Automative Industry." *European Journal of Operational Research* 199, no. 1, pp. 150–61.

Wilner, B. 2000. "The Exploitation of Relationships in Financial Distress: The Case of Trade Credit." *Journal of Finance* 55, no. 1, pp. 153–78.

Wu, W., O. Rui, and C. Wu. 2012. "Trade Credit, Cash Holdings, and Financial Deepening: Evidence from a Transitional Economy." *Journal of Banking and Finance* 36, no. 11, pp. 2868–83.

Wuttke, D., C. Blome, and M. Henke. 2013. "Focusing the Financial Flow of Supply Chains: An Empirical Investigation of Financial Supply Chain Management." *International Journal of Production Economics* 145, no. 2, pp. 773–89.

Yang, X. 2011. "The Role of Trade Credit in the Recent Subprime Financial Crisis." *Journal of Economics and Business* 63, no. 5, pp. 517–29.

Yang, A., J. Birge, and R. Parker. 2015. "The Supply Chain Effects of Bankruptcy." *Management Science* 61, no. 10, pp. 2320–38.

Yu, M. 2013. "Supply Chain Management and Financial Performance: Literature Review and Future Directions." *International Journal of Production Economics* 33, no. 10, pp. 1283–317.

Zhang, Q., M. Dong, J. Luo, and A. Segerstedt. 2014. "Supply Chain Coordination with Trade Credit and Quantity Discount Incorporating Default Risk." *International Journal of Production Economics* 153, pp. 352–60.

Zhang, B., P. Baeck, T. Ziegler, J. Bone, and K. Garvey. 2016. *Pushing Boundaries, The 2015 UK Alternative Finance Industry Report.* Nesta and Cambridge Center for Alternative Finance, February.

Online Sources

Association Française des Sociétes Financières. 2003. "Position of the ASF on the Third Consultative Paper of the Basel Committee,' www.bis.org, (May 20, 2015).

Atradius. 2017. *Atradius Payment Practises Barometer,* Spring. https://group.atradius.com, (May 02, 2018).

Baft-Ifsa. 2011. *BAFT-IFSA Product Definitions for Traditional Trade Finance.* www.aba.com, (October 20, 2017).

BNP Paribas. 2003. *Comment on CP3.* www.bis.org, (May 20, 2015).

Development Working Group. 2011. "2011 Report of the Development Working Group for the G20", *Summit in Cannes.* http://www.g20.utoronto.ca/summits/2011cannes.html (September 11, 2017).

EU Federation. 2017a. *Glossary and Translator.* https://euf.eu.com, (April 04, 2017).

EU Federation. 2017b. *EUF Yearbook 2016-2017.* https://euf.eu.com, (February 01, 2018).

Factors Chain International. 2017. *Statistics.* https://fci.nl/en/home, (September 11, 2017).

Fédération Bancaire Française. 2003. *Re: Consultative Paper n°3.* www.bis.org, (October 07, 2015).

Global Supply Chain Finance Forum. 2016. *Standard definitions for techniques of supply chain finance.* https://iccwbo.org/publication/standard-definitions-techniques-supply-chain-finance, (10/09/2017).

LiquidX. 2017. *LiquidX Advantage.* http://liquidx.com/liquidx-advantage

MarketInvoice. 2017. *Learning Center.* https://learn.marketinvoice.com, (October 10, 2017).

Office of National Statistics. *UK manufacturers' sales by product survey (Prodcom)*. https://www.ons.gov.uk/surveys/informationforbusinesses/business-surveys/ukmanufacturerssalesbyproductprodcom, (October 05, 2017).

Office of National Statistics. 2017. *Retail Sales Index*. https://www.ons.gov.uk/businessindustryandtrade/retailindustry/bulletins/retailsales/previousReleases, (15/05/2017)

Office of National Statistics. *Annual Business Survey*. https://www.ons.gov.uk/businessindustryandtrade/business/businessservices, (April 20, 2017).

Statistics Bureau of Japan. *Unincorporated Enterprise Survey*. http://www.stat.go.jp/english/data/kojinke/index.html, (February 12, 2017).

Statistics Canada. *Financial and Taxation Statistics for Enterprises*. http://www5.statcan.gc.ca/olc-cel/olc.action?objId=61-219-X&objType=2&lang=en&limit=0, (March 13, 2017).

United States Census. *Quarterly Financial Report*. https://www.census.gov/econ/qfr, (May 22, 2017).

Task Force on Finance Statistics. 2016. *Minutes*, n.18. http://www.tffs.org (May 23, 2017).

Websites

Bank for the Accounts of Companies Harmonized (Bach), https://www.bach.banque-france.fr/?lang=en

Board of Governors of the Federal Reserve System, https://www.federalreserve.gov

Bureau of Economic Analysis, Department of Commerce, https://www.bea.gov

EU Federation, https://euf.eu.com

Eurostat, http://ec.europa.eu/eurostat

Factors Chain International (FCI), https://fci.nl/en/home

Office of National Statistics, https://www.ons.gov.uk

Statistics Bureau of Japan, https://www.e-stat.go.jp

Statistics Canada, http://www.statcan.gc.ca/eng/start

U.S. Census Bureau, https://www.census.gov

World Bank, www.worldbank.org

About the Author

Lucia Gibilaro is associate professor in economics of financial intermediaries at the University of Bergamo and visiting professor at the Athens University of Economics and Business. She obtained her master's in asset management and PhD in banking and finance from the University of Rome "Tor Vergata." She has been visiting professor at the University of Essex. She is a member of the research center CISAlpino Institute of Comparative Studies in Europe at the University of Bergamo and she collaborates with the Real Estate Finance Laboratory at the University of Rome "Tor Vergata." She is the author of publications on asset-based lending, risk management, and fintech.

Index

Accounts payable, 46
Advances. *See* Loans
Asset-backed commercial paper, 68, 73, 94
Asset-based lending, 42

Bach categorization methodology, 16
Bank guarantee, 59–60
Bank instruments, 71–72
   factoring, 55, 57–58
   international trade, 57, 59–61
   self-liquidating loans, 54–55
   supply chain finance, 45, 60, 63–65
Bank payment obligation, 65
Berne Union, 2–3
Business relationships, 41–45

Capital goods, 83
Collection services, 59
Commercial letter of credit, 59
Commercial papers, 53–54, 65–66, 94
Concentration risk, 86–89
Conduit, 66
Consumer goods, 83
Contract enforcement, 34
Contractual dilution, 84
Corporate characteristics
   financial motivation, 38–41
   real motivations, 35–38
Credit risk framework, 75–91
   individual level, 77–86
   introduction, 75
   portfolio level, 86–89
   for trade credit financial instruments, 76–77
Crowdfunding, 54, 67, 69
Current suppliers, 38

Default, defined, 77–78
Default-related dilution risk, 82, 85

Default risk, 76–80, 90, 94
Defaulted debtor, 76
Delayed payments, pricing approach, 36
Delinquency, 78
Dilution risk, 76–77, 80–86, 90
   types, 82
Documentary letter of credit, 59

Economic development, 45–47
Economic sectors, 34–35
Empirical evidence, theory and
   business relationships, 41–45
   corporate characteristics, 35–41
   economic development, 45–47
   economic sectors, 34–35
   financial crisis, 48–50
   financial motivation, 38–41
   introduction, 33–34
   real motivations, 35–38

Factoring, 55, 57–58, 63
Financial crisis, 48–50
Financial motivation, 38–41
Financial supply chain management, 44–45
Financing instruments, 53–74
   bank, 54–65
   introduction to, 53–54
   market, 65–69
   self-liquidating exposure, 69–72
Firm type, segmentation, 16–20
Flexible supply chain finance services, 63
Forfeiting, 63

Generous cash discounts, 37
Global level, trade credit, 1–31
   firm type, segmentation by, 16–20
   industry segmentation, 6–16
   multidimensional segmentation, 20–30

G7 countries, trade credit in
  manufacturing sector, 9–10, 13
  sales, 8
  service sector, 9, 12, 15
  total assets, 6–7
  wholesale and retail trade sectors, 9,
    11, 14

Income analysis, 3
Industry risk, 66
Industry segmentation, 6–16
International factoring, 60, 62
International trade instruments, 57,
  59–61
Inventory management, 41
Invoice discounts, 54
Issuer credit risk, 66

Large firms, 16, 19–20, 23
Letter of credit, 59, 94
Letter of guarantee, 59, 94
Loans, 63

Macro-level, demand, 38
Manufacturing sector
  sales, 13, 25, 28
  total assets, 9–10
Market instruments, 71–72
  commercial papers, 65–66
  crowdfunding, 67, 69
  securitization of receivables, 66–67
MarketInvoice, 69–70
Medium-sized firms, 16, 18, 22
Menu of contracts, 43
Micro level, demand, 37
Multi-seller conduit, 66
Multidimensional segmentation, 20,
  24–30

Net term, pricing approach, 36
New suppliers, 38
Non-price discrimination, 36–37
Nondilutive credit, 84

Operational-related dilution risk,
  82, 85
Ordinary dilution, 82–84

Payables finance, 63
Peer-to-business, 67
Peer-to-peer lending, 67, 94
Pro soluto factoring transactions, 55
Procurement information, 79–80

Rating agencies, 65–66
Real motivations, 35–38
Receivables discounting, 63
Receivables Exchange, 69
Receivables financing, 55–56
Receivables purchase, 63
Relevance of debtor, 69–72
Reverse factoring, 45, 57
Rollover risk, 66, 67

Sectorial/geographical approach, 87,
  89, 91
Securitization of receivables, 66–67
Segmentation
  by firm type, 16–20
  industry, 6–16
  multidimensional, 20–30
Self-liquidating exposure
  legal characteristics, 69, 71–72
  operational characteristics, 72
Self-liquidating loans, 54–55, 93–94
Service sector
  sales, 15, 30
  total assets, 9, 12, 25, 27
Single-name measurement approach,
  87–90
Single-seller conduit, 66
Small firms, 16–17, 21
Small suppliers, 44
Special-purpose entity. *See* Conduit
Supply chain finance, 41–45, 60,
  63–65, 94

Trade credit
  business relationships, 41–45
  credit risk framework, 75–91
  economic development, 45–47
  financial crisis, 48–50
  financing instruments, 53–74
  global level, 1–31
  G7 countries, total assets, 6–7

international trade, 2–6
  role of, 3, 6
  theory and empirical evidence,
      33–52
Trade receivables, 49, 66
Traditional theory, 33
Turnover, 57
Two-part term, pricing
      approach, 36

2008 Global financial crisis,
      2–3, 6, 16, 25, 48, 52, 67, 73

Variable dilution, 84

Wholesale and retail trade sectors
  sales, 14, 29
  total assets, 9, 11, 25–26
World Trade Organization, 3

OTHER TITLES IN OUR FINANCE AND FINANCIAL MANAGEMENT COLLECTION

John A. Doukas, Old Dominion University, *Editor*

- *Global Mergers and Acquisitions, Second Edition: Combining Companies Across Borders, Volume I* by Abdol S. Soofi and Yuqin Zhang
- *Global Mergers and Acquisitions, Second Edition: Combining Companies Across Borders, Volume II* by Abdol S. Soofi
- *Risk and Win!: A Simple Guide to Managing Risks in Small and Medium-Sized Organizations* by John Harvey Murray
- *Essentials of Financial Risk Management: Practical Concepts for the General Manager* by Rick Nason and Brendan Chard
- *Essentials of Enterprise Risk Management: Practical Concepts of ERM for General Managers* by Rick Nason and Leslie leming
- *Frontiers of Risk Management, Volume I: Key Issues and Solutions* by Dennis Cox
- *Frontiers of Risk Management, Volume II: Key Issues and Solutions* by Dennis Cox
- *The Art and Science of Financial Modeling* by Anurag Singal
- *Escape from the Central Bank Trap, Second Edition: How to Escape From the $20 Trillion Monetary Expansion Unharmed* by Daniel Lacalle
- *Mastering Options: Effective and Profitable Strategies for Traders* by Philip Cooper
- *Understanding Cryptocurrencies: The Money of the Future* by Arvind Matharu

Announcing the Business Expert Press Digital Library

Concise e-books business students need for classroom and research

This book can also be purchased in an e-book collection by your library as

- a one-time purchase,
- that is owned forever,
- allows for simultaneous readers,
- has no restrictions on printing, and
- can be downloaded as PDFs from within the library community.

Our digital library collections are a great solution to beat the rising cost of textbooks. E-books can be loaded into their course management systems or onto students' e-book readers. The **Business Expert Press** digital libraries are very affordable, with no obligation to buy in future years. For more information, please visit **www.businessexpertpress.com/librarians**. To set up a trial in the United States, please email **sales@businessexpertpress.com**.

www.ingramcontent.com/pod-product-compliance
Lightning Source LLC
Chambersburg PA
CBHW062024200326

41519CB00017B/4920